How to Spot it & How to Fix It. Quickly!

TONY MESSER & PILAR TORRES WAHLBERG

THE LAZY WEBSITE SYNDROME

www.pickaweb.co.uk

First published in Great Britain in 2013 by Compass Publishing

ISBN 978-1-907308-23-9

Set by The Book Refinery Ltd
Printed and bound in the UK by Biddles, part of the MPG Books Group, Bodmin and King's Lynn

Contents

Contents

Introduction

Have you noticed how some businesses seem to dominate the top positions in Google? Have you ever stopped to consider what a top position in Google, or other search engines would mean for your business?

The truth is, the businesses that appear at the top of the Google listings are the ones that are attracting the lion's share of the traffic.

You may have spotted some of your competitors up there.

Imagine the advantages that these businesses are enjoying:

- ✓ Getting a huge amount of 'free' traffic
- ✓ Building huge customer databases, which enable them to up-sell additional products or services
- ✓ Building long-term, meaningful relationships with their customers
- ✓ They appear to be the 'go-to' authority websites that are respected by their peers
- ✓ Able to forge relationships with other market leaders

In short, these websites seem to be way ahead of the pack and have established a position of market dominance.

People often think that to attain this status on the Internet it would take years of hard work, and a huge advertising budget.

Whilst perseverance and advertising know-how are

important attributes, they are not the only way to get to the top in the Internet world.

There are thousands of well-established businesses, offering brilliant products or services that are just getting left behind by younger, leaner, smarter Internet-savvy start-ups.

The reason they are getting left behind is not because they are not great companies - they may well be great companies. They are getting left behind because the rules have changed, but either they haven't been informed, or they just do not understand them.

When we started out with our web hosting business www.pickaweb.co.uk there were no rules as such. The Internet was like the Wild West - a bit of a free for all! There was a degree of luck as well as judgement, just being in the right industry at the right time, you could say.

Since then, we have gone on to sell millions of pounds worth of services in extremely competitive markets.

When we started out in the spare room with a PC, we were up against some formidable competition that was flushed with millions of pounds of Venture Capital funding, at the height of the dot com boom.

So we have written this book to remove the guesswork for you. We have been down every possible blind alley that there is online, and we have the scars to prove it!

How to use this Book

In order to get the most out of the book we highly recommend that you complete the questionnaire at www.pickaweb.co.uk/lazywebsitesyndrome - just click on the questionnaire link. There is also a copy of it in this book. This will provide you with a percentage score, which will help to determine whether or not your website is 'Lazy'.

It is vital that you do this in order to get an understanding of where you are with your website right now.

Once you have your score, work through each section one by one, following the instructions. You can also access loads of videos and other help documents by clicking on the Resources link on our website. Simply go to www.pickaweb.co.uk/lazywebsitesyndrome

As you complete each section, you will address specific issues which are crucial to ensuring that your website starts to perform for your business.

Whilst the information contained in this book will give you a powerful plan for your website, there is one missing ingredient. You will need to take action. It will not be possible to achieve what you are capable of, without taking the necessary steps outlined.

We should also point out that this book is focused on natural search results rather than Pay Per Click (PPC) results. Whilst PPC is a vital marketing tool for many small businesses we have omitted this as PPC is a very broad subject in its own right and we will be covering this in another book.

Nothing in this book is very technical. Nothing requires a high level of expertise or experience; in fact anyone can do it! All that is needed is the desire to improve your business and the willingness to *take action.*

Who this Book will Help

This book will help *any business owner* who has struggled to create a dynamic Internet strategy for their business, or anyone who is just unsure as to which direction to head, in terms of the Internet for their business.

This book has been written with non-technical people in mind. Jargon has been kept to the absolute minimum and where necessary, we provide a range of videos and other materials to help you.

This book will help you to understand the real purpose of your website, and why most small business owners fail to get the most out of the Internet.

It will show you exactly where you are now, and it will present a step-by-step plan for the long-term improvement of your business, by ensuring that you create a dynamic Internet strategy.

This book will also help anyone struggling to understand how Social Media can be used for their business. It will help you to understand your Social Media Profile and Role, which will enable you to develop a long-term and consistent Social Media Strategy for your business.

One of the problems that we often see is that business owners either get frozen in the internet headlights, and just do not seem to be able to take the first steps, or they end up using a 'Scattergun' approach, never quite achieving the results that they deserve.

This book will allow you to understand what is required to create a dynamic internet presence for your business as well as a step by step approach to implementing this.

Before we jump in and look at the details, let's just step back for a moment to get some perspective on how the internet has evolved to date, and let's have a look at the direction in which it is moving.

The Three Stages of the Internet (to date)

Stage 1: Wild West (to 2003)

When we started our web hosting business www.pickaweb.co.uk back in 2000, it was basically a bit of a free for all, a land grab - the Wild West even! In order to achieve a good position in search engines, what was required was a bit of know-how in terms of setting up websites.

Search engines, like Google and Yahoo, did not have such sophisticated search algorithms as they do today. As a consequence, it was easier to 'game' the results by 'stuffing' Keywords all over a website - basically including the Keywords that people would search on, within the code and text of the site.

Although the business of search engines is to provide good quality search results, if the search results reward sites that display these characteristics, rather than those who genuinely reflect what people are searching for, then the overall user experience is not satisfactory.

Stage 2: Linking Strategies (2003 – 2008)

To address the issue of 'Keyword stuffing' and all the other 'On-Page' tricks, search engines started to include an element of recommendation in their algorithms by placing more of an emphasis on 'Off-Page Factors' and, in particular, *the number of links from external websites* to a website.

The term 'Off-Page Factors' just means those factors over which a website owner has less control. For example, we have control over the content of our websites, but we have less control over whether other websites wish to link to our website or not.

In effect, search engines introduced an element of peer-review into their algorithms, so that the top-ranked websites were the ones that had received most approval from external websites.

The reason that this was preferable was because 'Off-Page Factors' were more difficult to influence, and therefore, there was a greater degree of integrity in the search results.

To make it easy to understand, think of the links to your website being like a vote in an election. The winner will be the one with the most votes, i.e. links.

However, as with any system, if the rules of the game change, then the players need to adapt - and adapt they did!

Instead of concentrating on 'On-Page Factors', the emphasis moved to link building. As well as obvious tricks, like link farms (which were crude ways to get lots of links back to a site) a whole link-building industry sprang up to support people's efforts to get to the top.

A whole new range of strategies appeared, such as link wheels, paid links and article marketing, to cater for the needs of this rapidly growing market. To counter this, search engines introduced measures to reduce the effect of fake linking strategies, with the use of 'no-follow' links (if this is all sounding confusing, don't worry, we will come back to this later).

It was during this period that new Social Media sites, such as YouTube, Facebook and Twitter started to appear, and *'Blogging'* entered the language of the Internet. While many might not have thought so at the time, this was actually the next big bend in the road, and this is where we find ourselves today.

Stage 3: Social Media (2008 to the present)

Very few people (least of all the founders) could have imagined that a university community website, launched in 2004, could have mushroomed to create a network of hundreds of millions of active users across the globe, in less than a decade.

Quite simply, Facebook, Twitter, YouTube and all the other popular Social Media websites, have been nothing short of a game-changing phenomena.

But why is this? More importantly, what does this mean for you as a business owner?

Whereas the early years of the Internet were dominated by 'players', people who knew how to play the Internet game; today, the Social Media game is harder to fake. It is also open to new entrants, who just a few years ago, would not have been able to dream of the levels of success they now enjoy.

At its heart, it relies upon the consumer being much more willing to investigate their needs, and to look for alternatives than before. A key part of this process, which had previously remained offline, was now brought online, namely social recommendation and approval.

We are more than capable of blocking out unwanted messages from corporations competing for our attention, but that does not mean that we are going to stop consuming or buying. All that has changed is that we do it at a time of our choosing, and with organisations that we have researched. And increasingly, we are doing our research in one area above all others - Social Media.

So far, the Internet had been a disparate range of systems and approaches. Some worked, whilst others withered on the vine. But Social Media is where many of these systems merge, and it is no exaggeration to say, that in the near future, the companies that 'get' Social Media will prosper at the expense of those that do not.

A Powerful Plan to Take Your Business to the Next Level

So far, we have seen that the Internet goalposts are constantly changing. What seemed a sure fire way to get a top ranking just a couple of years ago, could actually be harming your website *now*.

It is no surprise that the Internet intimidates most business owners. It just seems to be a constantly moving target, and we all have so many things to do in our business lives, that it always seems to stay on the 'to-do' pile.

We have worked with thousands of businesses, and the types of comments we typically hear are:

- I just don't get technology - it's beyond me (technophobe)
- I've missed the boat and it's too late - I can't catch up (doubter)
- I haven't got an IT team to do it for me (delegator)
- I'll get round to updating it sometime soon (procrastinator)
- I just don't know where to start (just plain confused)
- This is going to cost a fortune! (Sceptical)
- My Website is pretty much perfect, thanks (complacent)

Do you find that you fall into any of these categories? If so, we have some good news for you. *We want to reassure you that this book is going to give you a blueprint for online success.*

Our approach is simple. We are going to fast-track you

through 20 easy-to-follow steps, which can be completed by anybody. They will be based around the three simple stages, which we will shortly introduce to you.

By the end of this book, you will have become a savvy Internet marketer. But that is just the beginning. We will provide you with a *powerful toolkit,* to ensure that you continue to maximise the potential of the Internet for your business.

Your website will no longer be a glorified business card. It will be a business-generating machine, which will put you *head and shoulders above your competitors.*

Simply put, by the end of this book you will be in the top two to three per cent of online entrepreneurs!

As we have said before, anyone can do it, and that includes you! The strategies and approaches that we will introduce to you can be implemented by anyone, regardless of their level of technical expertise.

You will never fear the Internet again, but your competitors will fear you! Let's get started!

Chapter 1: What is the Purpose of Your Website?

Before we do anything else, let's focus on a really fundamental question: 'what is the purpose of your website?'

If we ask this question to 100 people, we will probably get 100 different answers!

However, in its simplest form, your website exists for the sole purpose of performing the following three activities and NOTHING else:

- Prospect (getting more traffic, or visitors)
- Convert (converting visitors into customers)
- Grow (up-selling products and services to your customers)

Prospect

By 'prospect' we mean getting more people on to your website, and we need to make sure that your website *gets found.* As most people these days tend to search online via search engines like Google, we need to make sure that your website appears prominently in related searches.

In our experience, most people naturally tend to focus all their efforts on getting more and more *traffic* (visitors). Now, having loads of traffic (or visitors) is great, but traffic itself is not a means to an end. What you need to focus on is converting as much of that traffic as possible, into *paying customers.*

This is where focusing on conversion really pays dividends. The reason for this is simple; it is MUCH easier to increase conversions by 100% than it is to increase *traffic* by 100%.

Convert

By 'conversion' we mean creating a website that really appeals to your visitors. You need to be focused on giving them EXACTLY what they are looking for. You want to make it easy for them to initiate contact.

You want to make sure that you offer them lots of really useful information which will solve a problem or answer a question that they have. Ideally you should offer some of this information for free, *in return for their contact details* (so that you can then keep in contact...but more about that later!).

You also want to ensure that whenever someone initiates contact with you, their enquiry is responded to, without fail, and in a timely manner.

Useful Tip: *Customer contact* is like gold dust, and whenever someone comes into contact with your website, you should be doing everything (within reason) to convert them into *customers.*

Grow

Finally, once you have converted people, either into paying customers or onto a list of subscribers, you can then focus on how to 'grow' your relationship with them. This is not necessarily the opportunity for a hard sell though.

Take your time, and keep them informed of information that may be of interest to them, as well as introducing them to offers and related products or services you offer. The great thing is that this can be automated 100%, so that your website actually starts to work 24*7 for you, without you having to continually send emails from your PC.

If your website was doing this *for you,* imagine the difference that this would make to your business.

This book exists solely to enable you to understand and implement these simple, three-step strategies as quickly and as painlessly as possible, and we will go into more detail about each of these points in a few pages time.

Now that we know what a website *should* be doing, let's consider what a 'lazy website' looks like.

The Definition of a 'Lazy Website'

We would like to introduce you to Dave. Dave loves his job. He works as Regional Sales Manager, for a small firm that provides testing equipment to the motor industry. His role is to identify new business leads, close new sales, respond to sales enquiries, develop relationships with new and established clients, send out promotional and marketing material, and generally doing whatever it takes to bring in the business.

In short, Dave's role is to be the central lynch pin in his company's sales and marketing effort.

That is Dave's role.

Dave's actual *fulfilment* of that role is, shall we say, slightly different.

Never an early riser, Dave often strolls into the office later than anyone else, and then proceeds to ensure that he has his early morning coffee break, before cranking into action.

Once up and running, he seems to spend forever on his mobile phone 'developing relationships'. Nobody is ever sure what types of relationships he is developing, but they never seem to add up to much.

Of course, as he is on his mobile phone, he never seems to have time to take any incoming calls, and despite having a phone messaging system, he never seems too bothered about returning them.

Dave is really into Social Media, and after spending a couple of hours on Facebook and Twitter, to 'make sure he is up to speed on the latest industry trends', Dave often ambles out to an important business meeting with a 'key client'. These meetings, it must be noted, often seem to take place in the local pub.

After a relaxing two-hour lunch, Dave returns to the office to answer his emails. The trouble is that Dave just has so much incoming mail, that he never really seems able to work out who he has responded to and who he hasn't. As a result, Dave's use of email could best be described as a bit hit and miss.

Having answered his emails, Dave will often be the first to leave the office, usually on the pretence of another 'key meeting,' or to prepare for a customer presentation.

Maybe you know someone like Dave, or maybe you have worked with someone like him.

One thing is for sure; if you were Dave's boss you would not accept this behaviour for too long. You would expect a dynamic, goal-focused individual to fulfil that role, and you would expect them to be busily bringing in new customers and growing existing accounts. If that person were firing on all cylinders, your business would be flying.

The reason that this is the case is because many businesses fail to understand the missed opportunity that the Internet offers them.

The unfortunate truth is, that most small business owners still think that their website is like an online business card. It exists to give your address and email contacts to anyone who should need them. It has a few nice pictures and some bland text and that is pretty much it.

The harsh reality is that this just does not cut it these days. It is a degree of complacency, that is equal to letting someone like Dave, do pretty much as he pleases in your business and at your expense.

If your website is not working its socks off for your business, then you are really putting yourself at a serious disadvantage to more informed competitors.

In short, you could well be suffering from 'Lazy Website Syndrome.'

Most small businesses will just be grateful to have a website so that they can put a tick in the 'have a website' box. The problem is, that whilst just having a website was fine a few years ago, there have been a number of significant developments in recent years that have revolutionised how business is now conducted on the web.

That's the bad news.

The good news is that it is neither difficult, nor expensive to fix, and this book will prove *essential* for those who are keen to turn their lazy websites into ones that attract new visitors, convert them to paying customers and help you to retain them for many years to come.

The Lazy Website Questionnaire

OK, there are probably 15,000 things that could be done to improve your online presence, but the reality is that many small business owners have neither the time, know-how or the money to make the changes necessary.

It is for this reason that we have prepared a short questionnaire for you – to see what kind of website you have, and whether or not it is indeed a 'lazy website' It takes no more than three minutes to complete, but it is essential that you do, otherwise you will not know which areas to focus on, or what you could be doing differently. The answers are of the yes/no variety so there is very little thinking to do.

Just answer honestly. If you do not understand the question or we use words you do not understand, then it is safest to answer 'no' and move on.

Please do not proceed any further until you have answered the questionnaire in full. When you have finished, make a note of your score and keep it safe. We will return to this later. Have a go and we will pick up again when you are ready.

You can also find the questionnaire at: www.pickaweb.co.uk/lazywebsitesyndrome

Questionnaire:

1. I have a list of the best Keywords for my website.
2. I have created Metatags for every page of my website.
3. I have updated the file names (page names), Headings and the text of my website to include my Keywords.
4. I have signed up for Google Webmaster Tools and Google Analytics.
5. I know the Lifetime Value of a Client to my business.
6. I have a short and powerful Headline/Strapline on each page of my website which catches people's attention.
7. I have Customer Testimonials, Professional / Industry Accreditations and Key Suppliers Logos displayed prominently on the main pages of my website.
8. I actively build links to my website and I am comfortable performing this task (or a member of my team/an external company performs this task for me).
9. I use a chat facility on my Website.
10. I have a 24-hour phone line, which will be answered by a person and in my company's name even if I am not there.

11. I have a central helpdesk, which collects all of my emails, so that I can maintain contact with all customers' emails, and they are separated into relevant queues (e.g. sales, post sales, accounts and support).
12. I use Video on the home page of my website.
13. I have a Company Blog.
14. I have set up Google Alerts on my strongest Keywords, my company name and related industry Keywords.
15. I have written an eBook, which I offer for free via my website.
16. I use an email-marketing tool such as MailChimp, Aweber, Active Campaign and Constant Contact.
17. I have a sequence of follow-up emails for prospects (i.e. not clients yet) and existing customers.
18. I have a mobile friendly version of my website.
19. I have a Marketing Calendar, which I use to plan monthly offers to all of my customers and prospects on my lists.
20. I understand Social Media and I actively use it to generate interest in my business. I am active on a regular basis on Social Media platforms such as Facebook, Twitter, LinkedIn, YouTube and Google+.

Do You Have a Lazy Website?

How did you get on? At this stage, if you scored over 75% then you probably do not need this book! Well done, you are probably well on your way to being a leading player in your (online) sector and you probably just need to focus in on the questions that you didn't answer 'Yes' to.

However, in our experience, the vast majority of website owners will score less than 50%, and in many cases they will be less than 25%. If this is the case then unfortunately you do, in fact, have a 'Lazy Website'.

We are sorry to be the bearer of bad news, but accepting where you are is the starting point. If you find yourself in this position, please do not fret about it. Help is at hand!

Before we start to fix things though, let's take a couple of moments to consider what makes a website 'Lazy'.

What Makes a Lazy Website?

A 'Lazy Website' is quite simply one which is not earning its keep. It is just letting you down, in the same way that Dave would be if he were your Sales Manager. The reason it is important for you to understand this, is to help you visualise the missed opportunities available to you.

As we said earlier, your website only needs to perform three tasks for you. These are:

1. Prospect (get more traffic or visitors)
2. Convert (convert visitors into customers)
3. Grow (help you develop a long-term and profitable relationship with your clients)

Let's consider the questions that you have just answered, and let's see how they relate to each of these points. Don't worry if some of the terms we use sound a bit foreign to you at first, we will be explaining each one, and what they mean as we go through the book, and we will be providing you with many useful resources to help you along the way.

Prospect

By prospecting, we simply mean getting people to visit your website. As most people will find your website via Search Engine Results Pages (or SERPS for short) such as Google, then you need to make sure that your website is set up correctly.

First, you need to make sure that you have identified the best Keywords (terms that people enter into search engines to find something) that fit your business.

Next, you need to make sure that you include these Keywords into the code of your website (these are called Metatags) and that you update the page names of your website so that Google can categorise you correctly.

Before you rush out and start promoting your website, it is vital that you understand how much traffic you are getting and where it is coming from. This can be achieved by using Google Analytics.

Once you have your site set up, you can then start actively promoting it, by building links from other websites. You can start using Social Media and Blogs to help you to attract more interest (don't worry if you are not sure how to do this, it is all explained later on).

When you write a Blog, you will need new content to write

about. Google Alerts is a great way to get inspiration if you get writer's block.

Finally, the world is going mobile, so a *mobile friendly* version of your website is essential to make sure you do not miss out on that extra traffic.

Convert

OK, you have knocked your website into shape, and search engines are starting to take notice of you because you have given it a helping hand. You can see the number of visits per day increasing steadily.

Now is the time to focus on converting these visitors into customers!

The first thing to address is the 'Headline' of your website and the supporting text. Once you have your visitor's attention, you need some compelling text, to inform them 'what's in it for them'.

When that is established, and your visitor is interested in what you offer, you now need to demonstrate credibility, integrity and experience. You want to establish yourself as a safe pair of hands in the mind of your audience, so that they stay around, rather than heading back from where they came. Customer Testimonials, supplier logos and industry or professional accreditations or awards will help you to achieve this.

Perhaps they have questions? Perhaps they want to speak to someone? Maybe they feel a bit nervous about phoning you?

You could address this with a Live Chat facility, which allows you to engage on a personal level with someone who previously would have been just a number on your daily visitor stats.

Maybe your visitor prefers to browse out of hours or at the weekend. Not a problem. Unlike your competitors, you can use a 24-hour live answering service. This then means that your calls are always answered politely in your company name. The caller is much more likely to leave a message than if they get through to an answerphone. Just think how impressed they will be when you call them first thing on Monday morning! Congratulations, you have a new customer!

Alternatively your visitor prefers email. They are emailing many different potential suppliers for quotes. However, their email to you could be received by your central helpdesk, which, if used, immediately sends out an auto-responder from you, with a unique ticket number. How impressed will they be? Their enquiry requires several email responses, and you never fail to respond.

Your competitors? The email stays unopened in Dave's inbox!

If a picture paints a thousand words, what does a video do? Imagine this scenario: Your visitor initially notices your video standing out in the search results with no other competition. Intrigued, they click on it and they watch the video which has a link back to your home page, where they view your short, informative video, which tells them exactly how they will benefit from your service. Because this new visitor likes to see a human side to a company, they stay to find out more about the services that you offer.

They also see that you have a free eBook on offer for them. Not surprisingly, you know what questions your visitors will have on their minds and the title of your eBook clearly reflects this.

Now you have their full attention, they request a copy, and their email address is added to your auto-responder system. Within seconds they are reading through it, and discovering the answers to the questions they had on their mind.

Grow

You are now in a position to start a long-term relationship with your prospect or client. You can do this by automatically sending several personalised, informative and helpful emails. To your prospects it appears as if you have personally taken the time to email them.

This will send a powerful message to your prospect or customer: "We are here and we are ready to serve you. You can trust us because we are a professional company, we are willing to give you free information, and we understand your biggest challenge."

See how easy it is to impress your potential customers? Adding relevant follow-ups will almost certainly tip that balance, and you will be surprised at just how effective this is in gaining more customers. In this case, they decide to use your services. Congratulations, you have another new client! But that is just the start, understanding the real value of a client to your business means getting to grips with their overall 'Lifetime Value'. In other words, *the total amount of money they spend with your business, over a period of time.*

In order to ensure that you maximise the 'Lifetime Value', you can create a dynamic Marketing Calendar that guides you through each month, and provides the on-going discipline that will ensure that you take your business to the next level!

When you have this in place, you are on the path to ensure that your website delivers high profits to your business for many years to come.

If all of that sounds too much, or too exhausting, then we would like to reassure you that it is *all achievable and realistic.* This is the reason we have written this book and during the next few chapters, we will show you exactly how to achieve this.

However, if you really feel that you need a helping hand, or you simply don't have the time to implement these key strategies, then don't panic! We offer a wide range of Internet Marketing Services which will allow you to quickly transform your website into a Powerful Tool for growing your business. Please check out the Services link at: www.pickaweb.co.uk/lazywebsitesyndrome for more info.

For the rest of you, let's get started!

Chapter 2: Step 1 - Prospect

Keyword Mastery

Why Keywords are so Important

Whilst Google and other search engines are extremely powerful and complex systems, they do have their limitations. The main one is, like all computer systems, they need humans to provide them with data in order for them to process this into meaningful information.

Your Keywords are your opportunity to tell search engines exactly what you do, and influence how your site is found in searches.

In our experience, having worked with thousands of businesses, the people who understand this concept, and spend some time choosing the right Keywords and using them properly, are the ones that have the best chance of succeeding.

Unfortunately, it is also our experience that the vast majority of small business owners will either miss this step entirely, or make very little effort in getting their Keywords in place.

In fact, it is estimated that up to 30% of your position in search engines can be influenced by these 'On-Page Factors'.

JARGON BUSTER: *'On-Page Factors' – Keywords are a component of 'On-Page Optimisation Techniques' or 'On-Page Factors'. This just means that they occur on your website or 'On-*

Page'. Off-Page Optimisation Techniques are less easy to control because they happen on other people's websites, but we will come onto that in a moment.

Even if you do not choose exactly the right Keywords, you will still give yourself a much better chance of online success than if you ignore this step.

The great thing is – it is really EASY if your follow our step-by-step approach.

What are Keywords?

I am your customer, I don't know it yet, but I need the thing you have to offer. Let's say you have a pet-grooming salon in London, and I have a gorgeous spaniel that needs grooming, and I live in Notting Hill. More than likely, I am going to go to my favourite search engine and look for a dog grooming service in the local area.

When I go to Google and I type something into the search box, that is a Keyword, no matter how many words I use.

Here are some examples of Keywords I'm likely to type in:

- Grooming
- Dog groomer
- Pet salon
- Pet salons in London
- London dog grooming

All of these are Keywords, even though some are phrases.

Here are some things I am not very likely to type in:

- Cut
- Best
- Spaniel
- Shampoo

These are not good Keywords because they are too general. When people are searching for something, they tend to be quite specific and try to describe exactly what it is they are looking for. Basically, the best Keywords for your website are the ones people are *actually going to type into search engines.*

The first step is to brainstorm, and make a list of likely terms your prospect will use in the search box. You could ask your customers, "If you were going to search for a dog groomer online, what would you type in?"

Refine Your Keywords

Once you have prepared an initial list, you can use a Keyword Suggestion Tool to give you more ideas.

We have prepared a list of useful tools to help you; Go to www.pickaweb.co.uk/lazywebsitesyndrome and select the Resources link for more information, useful hints, tips and videos that explain exactly what you need to do.

You can also use Google's Free Keyword Tool at https://adwords.google.com/select/KeywordToolExternal to see if there are any extra words or phrases that you can add to the list.

Useful Tip: When searching, we recommend that you configure the search to reflect your own country and language, and also for laptops and PCs. You can do this using the options below the search box.

For example, if you were targeting the UK market then you would set it up as follows:

- ✓ Locations: United Kingdom
- ✓ Languages: English
- ✓ Devices: Desktops and Laptops
- ✓ Competition, Global and Local Searches

When you enter the Keywords, you are presented with a list of Keywords with several Headings: **Keyword, Competition, Global Monthly Searches, and Local Monthly Searches.**

Competition: In this row we are presented with Google's view on how competitive this Keyword is. This is based on how competitive this Keyword is for Pay Per Click rather than natural. While they are not based on the natural listings that we are interested in, they are a good guide as to what we are trying to achieve.

JARGON BUSTER: *Pay Per Click vs. Natural Listings. In Google's listings you will see that some of the results at the very top of the page, and on the right hand side say 'Ads relating to...' These are called Pay Per Click adverts. Basically, you as an advertiser pay each time your advert is clicked on. These are different from the main listing in the centre, which is free.*

Global Monthly Searches: In this row we can see how many searches are performed each month across the world. This is important if you are targeting customers in countries other than your own.

Local Monthly Searches: In this row we see the total number of searches each month in your country (NOT in your town, city or region).

Initially, you could have a huge list, but now you want to narrow down to the five or ten strongest Keywords.

The Perfect Keyword

In an ideal world, when narrowing down your search, you would select Keywords which have the following characteristics:

- High volume of traffic
- Little competition so that we have a good chance of getting a top listing
- Intent – a high degree of certainty that the person browsing wants what we are offering

Unfortunately, we do not live in a perfect world, so just follow our step-by-step approach to identify the best Keywords for your website.

Long Tail Keywords

Some Keywords are extremely competitive. These tend to be single words, e.g. hosting, domains, football, and insurance. It might be extremely difficult to get a good ranking on these Keywords because there is just so much competition.

However, there are also 'Long Tail Keywords', and these typically consist of several words, e.g. London dog groomer,

UK WordPress Blog Hosting. These can be advantageous to use because they have less competition, and can often drive more qualified traffic to your website. When compiling your list, you should aim for a mix of the more competitive terms with the Long Tail Keywords, which have several words to ensure that you are broadening the net for potential browsers.

Below are a few examples of Long Tail Keywords in different areas:

- ✓ Lithographic and digital printers Exeter
- ✓ Dog friendly hotels in Edinburgh
- ✓ Vegetarian Restaurants Central London
- ✓ WordPress web hosting UK

Eliminate High and Low Traffic Keywords

Your initial list of Keyword ideas will probably contain 40 or 50 results. The first thing to do is to eliminate the really High Traffic Keywords. The reason for this is that realistically, we probably will not be able to get quick results. Remove any Keywords from the list that have monthly searches in the hundreds of thousands or millions.

By now, you will have refined your list down to a more realistic number - say 20 or so. If you find that you have more, no problem, just continue to drill down. Any less, and you will probably need to go back to your initial list and see if you can identify any more.

Now that we have eliminated the really High Traffic Keywords (where we may not see any action for some time) and any Low Traffic ones (where there just isn't any action) we can start to really analyse the remainder in a logical manner.

Eliminate Time Wasters

Often you will find Keywords that are related to searches, where people are looking for information rather than a specific product or service. Typically these will be prefixed with the following:

- How do I...?
- How to...?
- What is...?

Generally speaking, when people enter these types of Keywords, they are looking for information, rather than looking for a product or service. For this reason, we should initially remove these Keywords from our list, as we want to focus on targeted traffic, where people are really interested in what we have to offer.

Eliminate High Competition Keywords (Slow Method)

Imagine that you are setting up a physical shop in the centre of town. You are probably going to be squeezed out by the big, more established shops, which have larger budgets and a wider range of products, etc.

It is exactly the same online, and we can avoid this by using the following, easy technique.

In Google, perform a search on each of your Keywords. Click on the first page that appears in the listing, go to www.prchecker.info and perform a search to identify their Google Page Rank.

JARGON BUSTER: *Page Rank is the way that Google determines the importance of a website in an easy to understand numeric way.*

A website with Page Rank of 0 (zero) is either brand-new or is not ranked very highly by Google. A website with an 8 or a 9 is one of the giants of Google like Facebook or DMOZ.

Go through each website that appears in the first 10 places, and keep a note of the Page Rank for each website. Add the 10 Page Ranks together, and then divide by 10. This will give you an average page rank for a website listed on page one of Google for that Keyword (if you are not comfortable doing this then just watch the videos on our Resources page at www.pickaweb.co.uk/lazywebsitesyndrome).

Let's illustrate that so that you understand. Let's imagine that you have selected the Keyword 'dog grooming Notting hill' as your Keyword. First, go to Google and perform a search on 'dog grooming Notting hill'.

Next, go through each of the 10 websites listed on page one of Google and do a check on the page rank of their home page using http://www.prchecker.info

You will then see a list like this (remember this is just an example):

Website 1: Page Rank = 4
Website 2: Page Rank = 3
Website 3: Page Rank = 2
Website 4: Page Rank = 3
Website 5: Page Rank = 2
Website 6: Page Rank = 2
Website 7: Page Rank = 1
Website 8: Page Rank = 2
Website 9: Page Rank = 1

Website 10: Page Rank = 0

Now you just need to add all of the Page Ranks together. In our example above the Total Page Rank = 20.

Once you have the total, divide this by 10 (because there are 10 websites listed) to calculate the Average Page Rank. In this case we divide 20 by 10 so our Average Page Rank is 2 (i.e. 20 divided by 10 = 2).

Now work through your list, and assign an average Page Rank to each Keyword. To do this, just add the total Page Rank for each page listed on page 1 of Google and divide by 10 (ignore Wikipedia/newspaper and other High Rank pages if you see that they are not competition pages). This will give you an average for the competition for page one.

Once you have your score, see the next section, which shows you how to interpret it. We will also show you a really *fast way* to get these results.

Eliminate High Competition Keywords (Fast Method)

Now that you know how to do this, you may want to consider speeding up the process. A really great tool that you can use is called SEOQuake. It is a plugin for the Firefox Browser. If that sounds complicated then relax, it is really easy to set up.

1. First just do a quick search on 'Mozilla Firefox download' and install Firefox – it is just another Internet browser like Internet Explorer or Google Chrome. It only takes a couple of minutes to install.
2. Once you have Firefox downloaded and installed, do a search in Google for 'SEOQuake download' and

again, just follow the instructions to install SEO Quake.

3. Once you have SEO Quake installed, when you search in Google, you will notice that a line appears under the results with information about each web page listed in the search engine results. The one that we are interested in is the Page Rank or PR.

The great thing about using SEO Quake, is that you can instantly assess the competition as soon as the results appear on page 1 in Google. You will soon develop an instinctive feel as to whether there is a lot of competition or not for your Keywords.

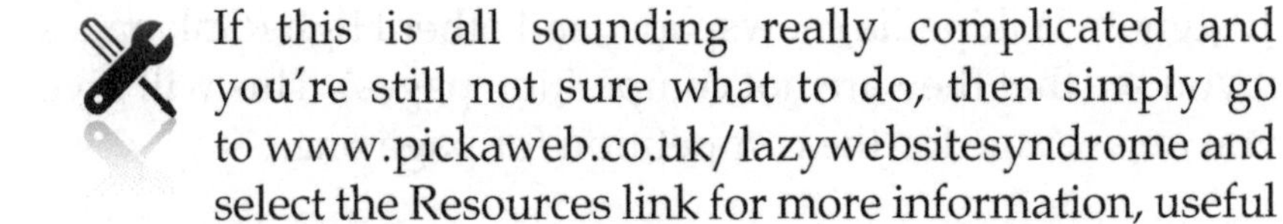

If this is all sounding really complicated and you're still not sure what to do, then simply go to www.pickaweb.co.uk/lazywebsitesyndrome and select the Resources link for more information, useful hints, tips and videos, that explain exactly what to do.

Choose Your Best Keywords

Next to each of your Keywords will be an average Page Rank score.

Below is a summary, which will help you to interpret the results and determine which ones to go for:

- Page Rank 0 to 2 - You will be able to get a top listing within a couple of months with a degree of effort.
- Page Rank 3 - You should be able to achieve a page 1 listing within several months of consistent effort.
- Page Rank 4 to 5 - it is a realistic longer-term aim to get onto the first page, but the higher listings will be dominated by well-established brands.

- Page Rank 6 and above – Avoid. You are up against the 800-pound gorillas of the Internet.

One More Small Step: Neighbourhood

The final step, once you have a final list together, is to go to Google, and do one final search to check which search 'neighbourhood' you are in.

For example, if you go to Google and type in 'pet salon' you will find that most of the choices on that page are about a game called 'Paradise Pet Salon,' and not about dog grooming shops. 'Dog groomer' displays dog groomers, and will also give you localised suggestions. In this instance, 'pet salon' would put you in the wrong search neighbourhood, so you need to ensure that you avoid using that particular Keyword.

How Many Keywords?

Initially just narrow your list down to six or so Keywords. If you offer a wide range of products or services then you will probably have more, but in the early stages we just want to keep focused.

We can add extra Keywords later, but in the early stages, half a dozen or so is more manageable.

Dave's view on Keywords

Remember Dave? He likes an easy life. If you choose the right Keywords, then you might end up attracting more traffic to your website. That would be good news for you, but bad news for Dave because he would potentially have to work harder dealing with all of the enquiries.

But we are not quite there yet, so Dave can relax for a while.

What we need to do now is to put our Keywords to good use on our website. That will make Dave sit up and think.

So let's just have a quick re-cap and look at your action points, and then we can proceed.

Action Plan

1. Prepare an initial list of Keywords - as many as you can think of.
2. Refine your Keywords using free tools like Keyword Map and Google Keyword Tool.
3. Focus on Long Tail Keywords.
4. Narrow your choice of Keywords to those that have good levels of traffic, lower levels of competition and intent to use your services.
5. Use SEO Quake to speed up the Keyword selection process.
6. Narrow down your Keywords to around six or so.

Need some help choosing your keywords? Looking for ways to get more traffic and more conversions? Why not take a look at our Internet Marketing Services. We offer a wide range of services to match all budgets and we will help you to transform your website into a Powerful Tool for growing your Business. To learn how we can become your trusted online partner please go to www.pickaweb.co.uk/lazywebsitesyndrome for more details.

Fine Tuning Your Site

Metatags and Headings

Now that you have a list of Keywords, you need to make sure that you include these on every single page of your website. This process is called 'optimisation', and because you control your website, and what content goes onto it, we call this 'On Page Optimisation'.

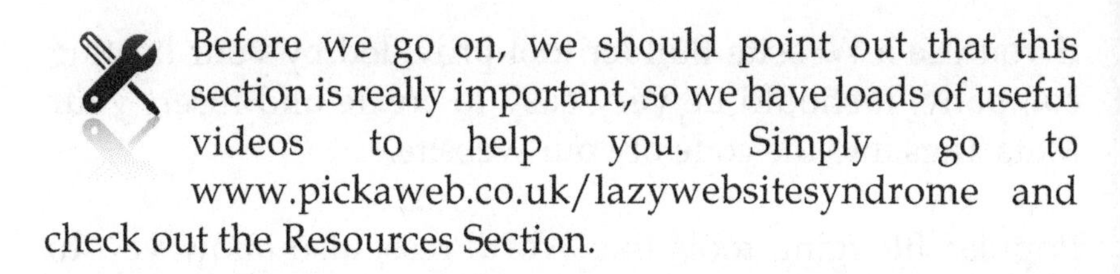

Before we go on, we should point out that this section is really important, so we have loads of useful videos to help you. Simply go to www.pickaweb.co.uk/lazywebsitesyndrome and check out the Resources Section.

Whilst your home page is really important, do not just concentrate all your efforts there. This is a common oversight! Remember you control what goes into your website, so give yourself every chance by looking at each page individually, and ensure that the Keywords you use reflect your content and what you're trying to promote.

For example, let's go back to our dog grooming salon. If we have one page that relates to a 'mobile grooming service' and another page for 'show grooming', then we should have specific Keywords for each page.

The key point here, is to make sure that you use different Keywords throughout your website. If necessary, create new pages to reflect the fact that you are targeting new Keywords.

JARGON BUSTER: *Metatags. Whilst these may sound*

complicated, they are actually quite simple. Metatags are the terms used to describe the code where your Keywords are located in the actual code of your website. The reason that they are important is that they enable search engines to categorise websites.

The most important ones are:

- Page Title Element
- Meta Description
- Meta Keyword

If you use a Website Builder tool provided by your hosting company, it should be very easy to create and insert your Meta Tags into the code of your website.

Popular Blogging tools like WordPress, also allow you to easily add your Keywords and they will automatically create the metatags for you.

Whether you are designing your own website using software such as Dreamweaver, or are using a designer for this, please create your Meta Tags as we are about to show you, and insert them into the code of your site, or pass them to your designer for inclusion in to your website's code.

To see some more detailed videos, with examples of how to upload your Keywords to your website using WordPress and other tools go to our Resources Page: www.pickaweb.co.uk/lazywebsitesyndrome

IMPORTANT: When you create your Metatags, make sure that you use different ones on every page. Avoid cutting and pasting the same ones over and over again on different pages.

Make sure that you customise them to reflect the content on that particular page.

Page Title Element

The Page Title Element is very important because it is used by search engines to categorise your website. You can see it at the top of any browser in the blue line at the top and you can see that this matches the first line in the search results.

JARGON BUSTER: *html. Hyper Text Mark Up Language or html for short, is the original programming language used for building websites. When you are on a website, right click with your mouse, then select 'View Source' or 'View page source' then you will see the html code – interesting, huh?*

For example, at the time of writing the html code for the Page Title Element for Amazon's home page looks like this:

<title>Online Shopping for Electronics, Apparel, Computers, Books, DVDs and more</title>

You need to create your Page Title Element as follows:

<title>Enter your chosen Title Keywords here – make them read naturally</title>

For example, in the case of our dog-grooming salon, they might use a Page Title Element like this:

<title> Dog Grooming, Dog Show Preparation and Mobile Grooming Services, West London</title>

You should create relevant Page Title Elements for each page of your website, and make them relevant to that page.

You should make your Page Title Elements up to a **maximum of 70-80 characters** (around seven to 10 words) and make them readable and understandable. Do not include any unnecessary jargon or filling-in words, and make sure they identify exactly what you do.

Useful Tip: Use your strongest Keywords as the first Keyword in your Page Title Element. Going back to the previous example, for the page relating to dog grooming make sure that 'dog grooming' is included first.

Meta Description

The Meta Description describes the content of a particular page, but in a little more detail, and is used by search engines to provide a summary of that page in the listings. Again, if you go to Google and do a search you will see that Meta Description appears on the second and third lines of each result in plain text.

You should use between 20-30 words, but do not use more than 180 characters in total including spaces. It should read naturally, and be customised to the particular page that you are working on.

You need to create the Meta Description as:

<meta name="description" content="Enter your summary here. Make it read naturally and customise it to the particular page that you are working on. No more than 30 words maximum.">

For example, in the case of our dog-grooming salon they might use a Meta Description like this:

<meta name="description" content=" The West London Poodle Parlour is an award-winning dog grooming salon. We offer high quality services both in our fully fitted salon and at your home.">

Meta Keywords

The last type of Metatags are the Meta Keywords. Unfortunately Meta Keywords have been subject to abuse, by people trying to trick search engines, and as a consequence they are not given much weighting –you can include them for completeness although you don't have to. If you do then use three or four of your best Keywords (including phrases) - but this time round they do not have to read naturally - you can just list the Keywords or phrases without creating natural sounding sentences. Again, you should customise them to make them relevant to the page you are working on.

You need to create the Meta Keywords as follows:

<meta name="keywords" content="Enter your summary here. Up to 30 of your best keywords and make them relevant to the page you are describing">

Here is an example:

<meta name="keywords" content="Dog Grooming, Dog Salon, Mobile Dog Salon, Pet Parlour ">

Headings

Now that you are familiar with html in terms of Metatags, we need to introduce another important piece of html, but this one is much easier to understand. On your page, you can help search engines to understand the structure of each page by using Headings.

Without structure, search engines find it hard to 'understand' your page. All you are doing is helping them.

There are six types of Headings. These Headings are called H1, H2, H3, etc. all the way up to H6.

If you have ever used a word processing tool like Microsoft Word, and you are familiar with using Headings, then this is very similar.

While there are six Headings, there are only three that you need to be familiar with - H1, H2 and H3, and you should try to use these on each page for maximum effect.

The html code for the Headings is really easy. All you need to do is to use the following examples:

<h1>Enter your heading here</h1>
<h2> Enter your heading here </h2>
<h3> Enter your heading here </h3>

For example, if you were using the Keyword 'Dog Grooming Services' then your H1 html heading would look like this:

<h1> Dog Grooming Services </h1>

On your actual website your heading would look something like this:

Dog Grooming Services

You then need to repeat this for the H2 and H3 Headings.

When you are creating your Headings, please resist the

temptation to just 'stuff' them full of your Keywords, as this looks unnatural. In the next section we will look at text in more detail, but the point to remember here, is that your Headings should include Keywords in a natural context. For example, rather than saying 'Dog Grooming Services' three times, maybe you could use three of your best Keywords as follows:

H1 Heading - The Friendliest Dog Grooming Services in London

H2 Heading - **Try our Home Dog Grooming Service**

H3 Heading - We also do Competition Dog Grooming

The important thing is to use Headings and to use your Keywords as naturally as possible.

Internal Link Structure

It is important that whenever you link to other pages in your website that you include your keywords in the link. This is referred to as 'Anchor Text'.

The reason for this is simple. When Google finds your website it looks for links to other pages to index. Remember that we mentioned earlier that On Page Factors are easier to control. This is a good example of this.

To give you the rationale behind this and to give you a real world example, imagine that you have an office furniture business in London. You have done your keyword research and you are trying to get a good position for the keyword term "office furniture London" for your website.

In this case, "office furniture London" would appear as part of your title, your keywords and the description metatag.

Make sure that you're clear *which keywords or phrase you want to link for.* You must make sure that these appear as text in your link and when selected you are taken to the relevant page on your website. You mustn´t just use any old words - you must use the keywords that you have identified. These are called the 'Anchor Text'.

Any links that you create to other pages in your website should include your main keywords in the Anchor Text.

This is really important.

The Anchor Text must say the keyword or phrase you're trying to get a ranking on. In our example, the link must include the keyword "office furniture London" and when you click on this, it must then go to your office furniture page.

In our example the html for the link would look like this:

<a href="http://www.YOURDOMAINNAMEHERE">Office Furniture London</a>

Dave's View on Metatags and Headings

Well, Dave thought that getting a list of Keywords together was bad enough, but putting them on your website using Metatags? You are asking for trouble. He will be in to see you for sure to tell you that he just can't handle all of these new enquiries!

But this is just the start. Next, we are going to make sure that we put our Keywords to even more use in our website.

Before we do that, let's just have a quick re-cap, look at your action points and then we can proceed.

Action Plan

1. Create Metatags for EVERY page of your website and make sure that they are all different - do not just cut and paste from page to page.
2. For the Page Title Element use your strongest Keywords first, make them read naturally and use between 70 to 80 characters (7 - 10 words).
3. For the Meta Description, use up to 180 characters (20 - 30 words) make it read naturally and be relevant to the content on that page.
4. For completion add the Meta Keywords - three or four Keywords separated by commas.
5. Add H1, H2 and H3 Headings on every page and include your Keywords in a natural context.

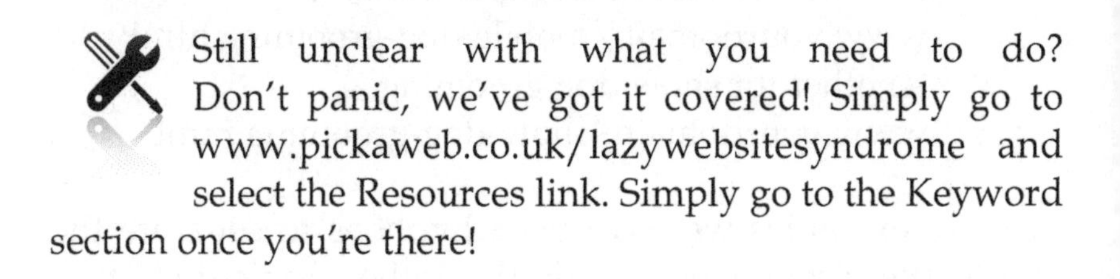

Still unclear with what you need to do? Don't panic, we've got it covered! Simply go to www.pickaweb.co.uk/lazywebsitesyndrome and select the Resources link. Simply go to the Keyword section once you're there!

Updating File Names and Text

All we mean by this is that we need to change the page names (URLs) of our website.

JARGON BUSTER: *URL. Techies love to refer to the address of website pages as Uniform Resource Locators or URLs for short.*

Using the dog grooming example again, let's say that you offer, 'mobile dog grooming' as well as 'show dog grooming'. You could have one page on your website that describes both of these services, but the problem is that you might be in danger of spreading yourself too thinly for search engines.

A better approach would be to build a page for each service, and to name each page based on each Keyword as follows:

- ✓ A page for your salon: www.yourdomain/dog-grooming-salon.html
- ✓ Another for mobile dog grooming: www.yourdomain/mobile-dog-grooming.html
- ✓ Another for show dog grooming: www.yourdomain/show-dog-grooming.html

In these examples we have used hyphens to separate the words. We recommend you do this rather than using other characters to separate your words. If you do not, you can get penalised by search engines for having non-reader friendly URLs.

The important thing to remember is that *you're including these all-important Keywords in the names of your pages,* so when someone searches using that Keyword, you are giving yourself a much better chance of appearing in the results, than if you just called your page 'services' for example.

Include your Keywords in Your Website's Text

Let's imagine a website that sells vintage jewellery. Having done their research, the owners have identified the Keywords 'jewellery,' 'antique jewellery,' and 'vintage jewellery.'

They've then written a short paragraph for their site:

Heartfelt **Jewellery** is your source for affordable vintage and antique **jewellery.** Whether you fancy retro bracelets from the '50s or elegant antique necklaces, Heartfelt **Jewellery** is the place to shop. We ship **jewellery** worldwide at one sensible shipping rate, and we pride ourselves on our fantastic service. Remember, all our **jewellery** is antique or vintage, so that piece you long for may not be here long. Browse our shop and place your order with our secure shopping basket!

The paragraph reads like natural English, but it also contains the Keywords several times. All the Keywords appear at the beginning of the paragraph, and they are fairly close together.

The paragraph also tells customers what they need to know in order to shop.

Now, let's look at another example and see if you can spot whether or not this is as good as the previous example:

Buy **antique jewellery, vintage jewelry,** and all **jewellery** from High Street **jewelers**, specialists in **jewellery**, antique **jewelry**, and **vintage jewellery.** We ship **jewellery, antique jewellery**, and hot **vintage jewellery** worldwide. Count upon us for your **jewelry, antique jewellery,** and **vintage jewellery** needs.

Can you see the difference?

Hopefully you will have noticed that this site is trying to trick search engines. These site owners are writing solely for search engines, not for their customers. This is what is referred to as 'Keyword Stuffing' or 'Keyword Spamming'.

Another sneaky trick is to use several different spellings of the word 'jewellery' in order to catch people who use different spellings, or who have misspelt something.

This looks suspicious to search engines, and it looks odd to human visitors.

Overall, you should aim for *two to three percent Keyword density* in your text, so for every 100 words, your Keywords should appear two or three times. Do not get too hung up about this though. The main thing is to make sure that you strike a balance between when to use your Keywords, and when not. The more you do it, the better you will get at it.

Dave's View on URLs and Text

Dave knows he has a fight on his hands now. Keywords, Metatags, URLs, text... will you ever stop trying to get more potential customers for him?

Well, Dave is telling us that he is getting more enquiries, but maybe he is just saying this to get you off his back. Let's get some hard facts and find out exactly how many visitors you are getting to your website.

Before we do that, let's just have a quick re-cap and look at your action points and then we can proceed.

Action Plan

1. Update every URL on your website (except your home page) to make sure that they include your keywords.
2. Use hyphens (-) if necessary to separate the words.
3. Change any bland or non-Keyword URLs e.g. mywebsite.com/services to Keyword rich URLs e.g. mywebsite.com/dog-grooming-services.
4. If necessary add new pages for different services & make sure that the URL includes the relevant keywords.
5. Rewrite your website's text to include your Keywords, in a ratio of two to three percent of the total on a page. Ensure that your text reads naturally and avoid stuffing your Keywords in.

For more information and useful hints, tips and videos please check out our Resources Page at www.pickaweb.co.uk/lazywebsitesyndrome

Google Webmaster Tools and Google Analytics

Sign up for Google Webmaster Tools

Google Webmaster Tools allows you to quickly see your website from Google's perspective. If there is a problem with your website's visibility in Google's database, it is important to find out about it as quickly as possible and this is the place to do it.

You can sign up for Google Webmaster Tools at www.google.com/webmasters/tools/ and it is totally free.

Once you have an account, the first thing you must do is to add your site. You do this by entering your website's address (URL) and then add a little bit of code that is provided for you. Upload this to your website's html, and Google will pick that up and confirm that you are listed.

To see how to do this, please check our video on Google Webmaster Tools on our Resources Page at www.pickaweb.co.uk/lazywebsitesyndrome

Next, you need to create an XML SiteMap.

JARGON BUSTER: *XML SiteMap. A SiteMap is just a way for you to tell Google what pages to index on your website. XML stands for EXtensible Markup Language. The difference between html and XML is that html is concerned with DISPLAYING data whilst XML is concerned with CARRYING data. I bet you're glad you understand the difference!*

There is a website that allows you to easily create your XML SiteMap at http://www.xml-sitemaps.com/

Once you have your XML SiteMap there is another task you need to do and that is to create a robots.txt file.

JARGON BUSTER: *Robots sound a bit complicated, but it is quite straightforward really. In order to be able to index your website the search engines use automated tools (or robots) to "crawl" your website. If you include a robots.txt file in your website then this helps them to understand which pages to visit and which pages not to visit. It is your way of controlling what they see and ultimately what they index in their search database. If you do not include the robots.txt file it doesn't do you any harm and a website that does not have this will still be crawled and indexed normally. It is really for completeness and to ensure that if you have pages that you do not want indexed then these will not be crawled.*

Rather than explaining this step by step, simply visit www.pickaweb.co.uk/lazywebsitesyndrome where we have prepared some resources for you in the Resources section.

As you get more confident, you will find Google Webmaster Tools really useful for bringing things to your attention, like duplicate content (which Google hates) and external links (we will get onto links shortly).

Sign up for Google Analytics

Now that you are getting to grips with SEO, you'll want to make sure that you can see how many people are visiting your website. Google Analytics is a pretty amazing set of tools that allows you to keep an eye on this, as well as a whole lot more.

JARGON BUSTER: *SEO. Search Engine Optimisation or SEO for short, is the term used to describe the practice of customising a* *website for maximum effect in search engines like Google. It consists of On Page Optimisation techniques (Metatags, etc.), which we have looked at previously, and Off Page Optimisation techniques (link building, etc.), which we will come on to shortly.*

You can sign up for Google Analytics at http://www.google.com/intl/en/analytics/index.html

Once you sign up, you will need to include the code that they provide, in all pages of your website that you wish to monitor. We recommend that you include it on all the pages of your website. It takes about 24 hours before you actually see any results, but that is all for now in terms of Google Analytics, we will be back to them later.

Dave's View on Google Webmaster Tools and Analytics
There is no hiding place for Dave. We can all start to see the traffic building up. Let's leave him with his new workload for a while, and focus on setting a few things up that will help us in the medium term.

Before we do that, let's just have a quick re-cap and look at your action points and then we can proceed.

Action Plan

1. Sign up for Google Webmaster Tools, submit your site and upload the code that they provide for you into your website.
2. Create a SiteMap & robots.txt file and upload to your website.
3. Sign up for Google Analytics and enter the code that they provide for you on all pages of your website.

Google Alerts

Now that you have established your Keywords it is worth signing up for Google Alerts at www.google.com/alerts – it is a free service, and it is a very easy way for you to set up alerts based on your Keywords, to be sent directly to you.

There are several reasons why you should do this. Firstly, as we proceed you will need to start building links to your website. One way to do this is to participate in the online 'chatter' in Blogs and other discussion forums.

If there is a posting on a relevant subject, Google Alerts will notify you, and you can join in the conversation. Fellow readers may notice you or you may be able to link back to your site (if the Blog allows this). Either way, you will be able to get a head start on others, and make sure that your comment gets noticed.

Secondly, as we move forward, we will cover Blogging, and we will show you why creating valuable content will establish you as an expert in your field. Creating content is easy for some, but for others it can be a drawn-out and frustrating process.

The great thing about Google Alerts is that even if you do not actually contribute to the online conversation, you can still get loads of great ideas and inspiration from others. Obviously, take care to avoid plagiarism, but do not be frightened to take inspiration and get ideas for your own content.

Finally, you will save yourself a lot of time, because instead of going out and searching for relevant content and Keyword mentions, you will get them sent directly to you. It is like having your own personal assistant out there searching for interesting and relevant content.

You can set Google Alerts to notify you when new content appears in News, Blogs, Videos, Discussions and Books. You can set it to notify you as-it-happens, once a day or once a week. You might find that if you set the system to as-it-happens it will give you too many results, but you can always adjust this later.

Dave's View on Google Alerts
Well, as long as you are not disturbing Dave, he is happy. But what Dave does not realise is that you are setting up a system to make sure that your company is going to be getting loads of mentions all over the Internet.

We will be looking at that in more detail in the next section, but before we do that let's just have a quick re-cap and look at your action points, then we can proceed.

Action Plan

1. Sign up for Google Alerts.
2. Have a cup of tea, you've earned it!

Link Building Mastery

What are Links?

What do we mean by links? Well, by links, we mean who is linking to your website.

Back in the good old days (2000 - 2003), it used to be enough to identify your Keywords and to include them in your website Metatags and text (explained earlier).

The problem was, that over time people developed ways of tricking search engines into thinking that their sites were more relevant and search-worthy than they actually were, so something had to change!

Links = Votes

To address this, the major search engines devised a way of ensuring that they protected the integrity of their search results. They did this by implementing a system based on the trust of a website. By trust, we mean how your internet peers view your website, and this ultimately translates into the number of times that links pointing to your site appear in other people's websites.

So, the more links you have to your website from other websites, the better chances you have of getting a good position in search engines. Try to think of a link as being like a vote for you. People are basically saying "hey, this is a useful website".

To start with, let's look at the importance of obtaining good quality links. In fact, you can probably expect that two thirds of your search engine ranking will be due to the number and quality of links to your website.

Link Building is a Gradual Process

Therefore, you need to start to think about creating these all-important links, but before we start there is a quick note of caution for you: Link Building is a process that needs to be done methodically, patiently and over time. You cannot go from 0 links to 1000 in one week, or you risk being penalised by the major search engines, and in extreme cases removed from their listings altogether! So if you see an advert for mass linking, please avoid the temptation - it could do you a lot of damage.

On the other hand, following sound and gradual link building techniques is crucial, and it is important that your link growth is as natural as possible.

Easy Wins - Directories

If you are just starting to promote your website, one of the best (and easiest) ways to get some good inbound links, is submitting your website to directories.

Directories are just online resources that categorise websites and provide a link back to them. They are not all equal though. Some are extremely well respected, and a link from them to your website confers a degree of trust. Others are just compiled lists of online resources and they do not really have much authority in the eyes of Google.

Having said that, directory submission is an easy task for

beginners, and as long as you take the time to check the directory, having a link from them is a positive thing.

To get you up and running we have prepared a list of the most authoritative Directories for you at www.pickaweb.co.uk/lazywebsitesyndrome Some of them are paid for, but they are definitely worth it if you have the budget, because they will link back to your site, which is what we are after.

Easy Wins - DMOZ - The Most Important Directory

Now that you have started doing a few Directory Submissions there is something very important that you will need to do as soon as possible - submit your site to the Open Directory Project, which is also known as DMOZ. The website address is http://www.dmoz.org

DMOZ is a multinational, multilingual directory, and the reason it is so important is that Google, and many other directories, use DMOZ as a source of information for their listings.

One really important feature of DMOZ, is that all the websites that are included are reviewed by humans, and therefore, a listing there demonstrates a degree of confidence in your website.

Either way, the key point is that you need to be included in DMOZ, and it is <u>very important that you follow the instructions</u> that we are going to show you now. You only get one bite at the cherry, so we are going to show you how to do it correctly using an easy-to-follow example.

Before we start, you must read the instructions at http://www.dmoz.org/add.html *carefully,* as they are for your benefit. Basically, they are drawing your attention to the fact that you must avoid certain techniques, which may be considered as Black Hat or underhand.

JARGON BUSTER: *Black Hat. As we mentioned previously, in the early days of the Internet it was a bit of a free for all. Search engines have, effectively outlawed the types of practices that would get you a high ranking back then. However, some people will still persist with these practices. These types of SEO techniques are referred to as 'Black Hat SEO'.*

Practices like submitting sites that have identical content, anything containing illegal material, sites with disguised URLs, for example, are not permitted. So you must play by the rules!

Next, because DMOZ is a Directory, it is based on Categories; this means you need to search through these to find the best place for you.

Let's use an example based on an online office furniture retailer who is based in London:

The first thing is to identify the strongest Keyword as we showed previously.

For the purpose of our example, we have identified the best Keyword to be 'office furniture London'. When at http://www.dmoz.org/ we then search for the Keyword - in this case 'office furniture London' - we can then see a results page for those words.

We click on that link and we are then taken to another page, where at the top we will see a link that says 'suggest URL' - once we have clicked on that, we can then suggest our site. At this point we refer back to the instructions that DMOZ provide.

Useful Tip: Make sure that the description is concise and accurate. You do not need to write a hard-sell advertisement.

On the website, DMOZ states that you should submit "an objective, well written description" and that is what you should aim for.

Once you have submitted your site, it can take months to appear. The reason for this is because *people* actually check your submission, rather than an automated check.

It all depends on the category that you have submitted to, as some are more competitive, and therefore have many more submissions than others. Overall, there are thousands of submissions at any one time, so you will need to be patient.

One final point: If you have already submitted once, do not do it again - you just have to be patient!

We have included a video, which shows you step by step how to submit to DMOZ. Simply go to www.pickaweb.co.uk/lazywebsitesyndrome and select the Resources link and then go to the link building section.

Easy Wins - Submitting to Google, Yahoo and Bing

When it comes to major search engines, Google is the top, so it makes sense to start here.

You can submit your website to Google at http://www.google.com/addurl/ and the great news is that it is very quick and easy.

Follow the directions exactly as stated:

1. First, enter the whole URL of your site, including http:// for example http://www.yourwebsiteaddress.com
2. Submit the homepage of your website, and no other pages.
3. Put your top two or three Keywords in the comments (optional).
4. Copy the letters you see into the box beneath the letters. This is a security feature called a 'captcha,' and is intended to catch automatic submissions by machines or computer programs, which Google does not allow.

There, all done, pretty easy, huh? Now in terms of timescales, you do need to be patient. It is impossible to say when you will appear in the search results. Sometimes it can happen in just a few hours, and sometimes it can take weeks to appear. The good news is that we are going to be showing you loads of great hints and tips for you to be working on in the meantime, to make sure that you do get listed.

You can submit your site to the other search engines in pretty much the same way. Yahoo and Bing each have a lower percentage of searches, but they are the next ranking search engines after Google. We have included the relevant links for Yahoo and Bing at www.pickaweb.co.uk/lazywebsitesyndrome - just select the Resources link and go to the link building section.

Easy Wins – Getting Listed Locally and Niche Listings

Some businesses are all set up to cater for a local community. Examples include; local taxi firms, cleaning services, childcare services, delicatessens, furniture stores, speciality shops, restaurants and all sorts of other members of the local community.

A growing number of your customers and clients will begin by checking your website, even if they complete their transactions with you by phoning or walking in. This is often referred to as "Research Online, Buy Offline" or ROBO for short. So, if your business has a physical presence, a store, office or shop front, then you will see the benefits of local listings *immediately*.

Now, if you want to sell to the world, you may be tempted to ignore local listings.

But here is why you shouldn't:

- You will get good local rankings faster than good general rankings. That is, you will appear at the top of the search engine results page faster using 'Birmingham guitar repair' than you will using 'guitar repair.' Since many people search that way, you might as well take advantage of it.
- Every listing you have is a link, and links are good for your ranking.
- Your presence in local listings makes search engines more likely to offer you to people in your area. With

geo-targeting, people in Birmingham who type in 'guitar repair' will be given Birmingham guitar repair services like yours first - but only if search engines understand that you are in Birmingham. Listings in local directories help search engines grasp that.

Important Local Listings

All the following directories offer free listings. One point worth noting is that in general, you must have a local address to be included.

- ✓ Google Places gets you on the map at the top of the page. You will have to confirm your listing by phone or post
- ✓ Yahoo Local requires a brick and mortar location, and will not list businesses that sell only online, even if you have a local address
- ✓ For Ask City, email askcitybusiness@help.ask.com with your information
- ✓ Localeze
- ✓ Thomson Local
- ✓ Touch Local
- ✓ City-visitor
- ✓ Yell direct, today's Yellow Pages

As with all listings, the key to success is to follow directions very precisely. Often, the directions seem needlessly complex and finicky. This is intentional; because the directories want to make the instructions so complicated that only human beings can follow them.

You should also search for local directories in your own city, and consider using your Chamber of Commerce and similar organisations, as they often link to the websites of members.

Easy Wins - Google Places - How to Get a Top Listing

If you perform a search which includes a town or city in the search term (e.g. 'Vets Glasgow') you will usually find that the first six or seven results will be highlighted on a local map, in the top right of the results.

These listings are shown because Google is trying to present the most relevant results to you. If you perform a few searches you should start to see a pattern appearing.

Can you spot it?

The sites which tend to get the highest listings have received Google reviews from their customers. If you click on one or two of the review links, you will be taken to their Google Places page where you can read them.

Anyone that has a Gmail (what was googlemail) account, or who has signed up for a Google service such as Webmaster Tools, Analytics, etc., and who is a genuine customer, can make a review of your services in your Google Places account. The more reviews you get, the more it will help your position in local searches.

However, a word of caution - it is not advisable to try to game the system. If you suddenly start to receive dozens of positive reviews, this may raise alarm bells at Google. At minimum, your account could be suspended temporarily, and at worst you could be banned altogether.

A far better approach is to check through your customer list and email several at a time (if they have a gmail address) and ask if they would care to review your website in Google Places. Send them a link to your Google Places Profile, which you can access at the top right of your profile (a small chain/link image.)

Consider sending to satisfied customers to get them to review you.

Again, we have included a video, which shows you step-by-step how to get the most out of your Google Places Listing at our resources page at www.pickaweb.co.uk/lazywebsitesyndrome just go to the link building section.

Easy Wins - Niche Directories

As well as Local Directories, there are thousands of little directories. Some are link farms - pages set up to facilitate link exchanges which you may want to avoid if they are just pages of lists - but many are the honest efforts of people in specific niches to provide useful information to others in their field.

As an example, if you are a musician based in the UK, the chances are that you use UKMusic.com, UK Music Directory, Musician UK, or EntsWeb. It is, for you, easier, more comfortable and faster to go to your specific directory than to use Google.

So, if you perform guitar repairs, it makes sense for you to list your services in directories that cater *specifically for guitarists or musicians in general.*

In your own field, you may already know of some good websites for the purpose. However, you can find more by searching with a string like this:

- Guitar repair "add URL"
- UK guitar repair "suggest site"
- Guitar repairs "add listing"

When doing these searches, ensure that you include the open and close ("") speech marks.

You will have hundreds of possible sites where you might choose to list your website.

Notice we said, "you might choose to?" This should not be automatic. Poor-quality links do not benefit you the way high-quality ones do, so you would be wise to look closely at the pages before adding your information.

Consider the following points before submitting:

- Is it a valuable site? Does it contain good content? If not, you do not need to be listed there.
- Is it relevant to your customers? Even if there are guitar repair links shown, it may still not really be a good place to list your guitar repair services. For example, if the listings were primarily of an adult only nature you would be wise to exercise a level of discretion and if you are not sure just move on to the next one.

Link Building Strategies

If this book had been written a year or so previously then it would probably have included a section on using techniques such as Competitive Link Building & Article Marketing as ways of getting links to your website.

The SEO Arms Race

However, the internet as a platform is still evolving and in terms of Search Engine Optimization, it is almost akin to an arms race, albeit a (usually) friendly one. One side (i.e. Google) creates a system which the other side (i.e. the rest of us) then tries to exploit for maximum benefit.

There is a period of relative calm where the SEO community looks for chinks in Google's armour. When they find these chinks the SEO high command will exploit these weaknesses to the full and gradually news of these techniques will filter out and everybody jumps on the bandwagon and tools are developed to support these efforts.

This can be seen by the 3 distinct phases of the internet (to date) which we described in the Introduction to the book:

Stage 1: Wild West (to 2003)
Stage 2: Linking Strategies (2003 - 2008)
Stage 3: Social Media (2008 to the present)

Competitive Link Building & Article Marketing belong very much in the "Linking Strategies" phase and we shall cover these briefly in a moment.

However, the important point here is that Google's most recent changes were the Panda and Penguin updates to their algorithms and in a nutshell Google "nuked" a number of - what had been until then - effective SEO strategies.

The reason for this was that Google considers the following as underhand ways of 'gaming' their results pages:

- Reciprocal Link Building (i.e. you link to me, I'll link to you)
- Paid for Links (i.e. I have a PR3 site & you can buy a link to your site on my home page for $50 a month)
- Competitive Linking (i.e. copying your competitors, link for link regardless of the type of page that's linking to them)
- Article Marketing (i.e. writing articles and distributing them in bulk to numerous article directories, in return for links to your website)

Never mind the quality, feel the width

The problem with these approaches was that link building had become a bit of a numbers game. It was more focused on the volume of links rather than the quality of links.

To address this, Google now places a much greater emphasis on social validity and approval. In effect they have set their system up to identify and reward genuine content creators who are interacting with others online. This is very much at the expense of those who are just re-hashing and recirculating low quality information in an attempt to trick the search engines.

The bottom line is that it is much more difficult to 'fake' real, intelligent human interaction than it is to create cheap, copied, regurgitated and low quality content or to simply copy your competitors' linking strategy.

So if we go back to our list above, the first two usual suspects *(reciprocal link building and paid for links)* are to be avoided. The only exception in terms of paid links, is if you are advertising on a related website (see below) or if you are paying to be included in a reputable directory such as Business.com or Best of the Web.

However, the last two *(Competitive Linking and Article Marketing)* are worthy of a little more inspection, because as in any arms race, old weapons can sometimes be brought up to date.

First, we'll take a look at these last two techniques in their previous forms and then we'll show you more up to date versions that you can use to your advantage without ending up in Google's line of fire!

Competitive Linking (v1)

In one of the Godfather films, Marlon Brando says: "Keep your friends close but your enemies even closer".

Well, the same goes here because competitive linking was effectively a way of keeping an eye on what your competitors were doing in terms of the links to their websites. All you then had to do was to copy this and hey presto you would move up the ranks.

Basically, the idea is that someone else has already done the homework for you - *your competitors.*

Isn't that great! We let them do all the hard work, and we can just jump on their coat tails.

All you would need to do was to use a tool like

http://www.opensiteexplorer.org/ to analyse where they are getting their links from, make a note of them and try to copy them.

You would create your anchor text (more on that in a moment) on your best keyword and you would relentlessly pursue the same links as your competitors.

The problem here is, you will find that in the vast majority of cases they are using a mixture of reciprocal links and/or paid for links. This now is a no-no as far as Google is concerned. If you follow them, then you are likely to end up in trouble at some point.

Now some of you may be thinking; "Well that's great. Our competitors can get away with all this underhand stuff whilst we have to play by the rules." This is a view that we can sympathize with, but don't worry. They may get away with this approach for a while, but soon enough they will appear on Google's radar and they will not have any choice but to change their tactics.

In fact, a cottage industry has grown up around having links removed from websites that may be harming your reputation in Google's eyes. These services are not free and the alternative is to contact all of these websites yourself to request link removals - a tedious waste of your valuable time.

So, if you are just starting out, or have limited exposure to link building, then you are starting with a blank canvas. Aim to follow the rules and soon you will be ahead of those competitors who are struggling to remove poor quality links pointing to them.

So, that said, how can you use competitive linking? Let's find out.

Competitive Linking (v2)

Whilst the idea of just copying your competitors' links is not really a long term strategy for you, there is an alternative which still allows you to let them do much of the spade work.

Rather than just imitating their linking strategy, what you can do is to look at their content strategy. By that, we mean see where they are posting their content to and what type of content they are posting.

Apparently Jimi Hendrix would take time out to see even low grade guitarists and when quizzed on this he replied that you never knew where you could learn something new.

Basically, he was always on the lookout for a new trick or a new angle on something that he had long before mastered.

If you apply this thinking to yourself, then you will have no problem in creating the all-important content that Google requires. As we will discover in the next section, your blog is going to become the centre of your online world around which your social media activity will help you to draw new visitors.

Useful Tip: You have to give Google what it wants. It does not want you to fake it or use underhand techniques. It wants you to be genuine & sociable. It wants you to share your knowledge with the community.

The Three 'R's' of Competitive Link Building

Did you ever get caught copying someone else by your teacher at school? Come on, admit it - we won't tell anyone! Your teacher probably noticed that you had the same answers as the person next to you. But what really settled it in their minds was the fact that you copied the wrong answers as well as the right ones.

This is the same online. If your competitors have got links from disreputable sites then you are best advised to avoid copying them.

If you are tempted to try the 'old school' form of competitive linking, then it is still a valid way to get links if you apply a degree of good judgement (as opposed to just copying their mistakes).

The key to this is to ensure that you exercise caution when you look at your competitors' linking strategies and analyse each link very carefully. The way to do this is to remember the three 'Rs' of Competitive Link Building. Let's show you what we mean.

When you have a list of sites that link to your competitors you need to be able to form a judgement quite quickly on the quality of that link. A good way to do that is to consider whether that site is *related, reputable* or **regional**. The following examples illustrate this:

Is the website **Related** to what you do? For example, if you are wedding photographer and your competitor has a link to their website from a building supplier's website or a hardwood flooring company then that is not related. In this case you would avoid. Don't be tempted by high Page Rank websites. Just move on.

Is the website **Reputable?** Is it a real company with a Company Registration number or a VAT/GST number? Does it have a contact us page with an address or phone number? If not, does it have a blog and how often is this updated and does the blog look like it is "owned and cared for" rather than just a load of random postings? Are there loads of other links from this website to other websites, i.e. are they clearly selling links? Try to use your judgement again and if the website is not reputable you are advised to avoid. Sooner or later Google will be on their case and you would do well to avoid them now.

Is the website based in your **Region?** When we say regional, imagine that a visitor found a link to your website on a website from a business that was in another country where they speak a completely different language and where you have no likelihood of doing business now or in the future. Would that link appear natural to the visitor? If the answer is no then it is best to move on.

Of course there will always be exceptions. Maybe you find a page linking to your competitor and they are a major supplier in your industry. If that is the case then that would be fine. But if your competitor is clearly getting links from all sorts of exotic websites in all sorts of different languages than they are probably just buying links and you should avoid copying them.

So in summary, just ask yourself whether the linking site is ***Related, Reputable*** *and* ***Regional.***

Again, we have prepared several videos to help you, and you can find these by selecting the Resources link at www.pickaweb.co.uk/lazywebsitesyndrome

Other Points to Consider with Competitive Linking

Anchor Text

Previously when we looked at On Page Factors and Anchor Text, we explained that it is important to use your keywords in the anchor text when linking internally to pages within your website.

Until recently this was also true of links from other websites to your website. People would go to all sorts of lengths to get their keywords included in the anchor text of the page that linked to them. However, this too has fallen foul of Google's latest updates.

The reason for this appears quite natural when you look at it from Google's perspective. Whereas they expect websites to link to other websites they expect it to happen in a natural manner. If you are trying to get a good ranking for a keyword such as 'Office Furniture London' it would be fine for you to use that anchor text within your own website. However, if someone was linking to you from another website would it be natural if they used 'Office Furniture London' in the anchor text? Probably not.

Sure, one or two like that are fine, but if you set out to get ONLY links with the anchor text 'Office Furniture London' then that is going to look strange to Google. They like to see natural linking patterns. For example they want links with your URL (i.e. your website's address) as the anchor text or maybe they want to see links with your company name as the anchor text.

For example, instead of using:

<a href="http://www.YOURDOMAINNAMEHERE">Office Furniture London</a>

A more natural link would be:

<a href="http://www.YOURDOMAINNAMEHERE"> www.YOURDOMAINNAMEHERE </a>

Mix the Target Page

Another point to bear in mind is that whilst your home page is very important, try to resist the temptation to target all of the links to your home page. Spread the links over other pages of your website too, so that you are giving more strength to the whole of your website.

This is called 'Deep Linking' and is a *vital strategy* for your long-term success.

Mix the PR

Finally, resist the temptation to only go for high PR sites. Obviously you will spot some great opportunities, but the whole process is a long-term game. Do not just look for the home run or the big hit. Try to get a good mix of links from high and low PR sites.

However, if you follow our advice, and our step by step plan, then you will be just fine. Of course, if you still feel that you need some help, then why not look at our Internet Marketing

Services. With us as your trusted partner you will quickly be able to transform your website into a Powerful Tool for growing your Business. To discover how we can help you get more out of your website just click on the Services link at www.pickaweb.co.uk/lazywebsitesyndrome for more details.

Article Marketing Is Dead!

In recent years, Article Marketing has been a staple form of link building for many Internet marketers. The basic idea is that you write a useful and informative article, upload it to an article directory and you include a link back to your website using your main keyword as your anchor text.

Hey presto, Google comes across your article, sees that lovely anchor text linking to your home page and pushes you up the rankings.

It gets better though. Rather than just writing one article, why not send it out to loads of different article directories and get loads of links back.

In fact, why not just enter it into a tool that will not only automatically distribute your article to hundreds of directories, but it will also rewrite the text (article spinning) as well as mixing up the Anchor Text for you.

Better still, why not just use a tool that searches for other blogs and copies their content automatically, re-writes it as your own for you and then does all of the above for you. How easy is that?

Can you see where this is going? This is what we mean when we talk about an "SEO Arms Race".

The reason that article marketing has become discredited is mainly because it was a victim of its own success and simplicity. The fact that everyone could easily do it, meant that somewhere along the line people would cut corners in terms of quality.

Add automatic article spinning tools into the mix and suddenly "Salt Lake City" becomes "Sodium chloride body of water town".

You can start to see why Article Marketing got a bit of a bad name.

The problem for Google is that its role is to provide people with the information they want and useful rather than something that has been copied and regurgitated endless times until it has had any meaning or sense stripped away.

Sure, some articles may be honest attempts to provide a solution to a particular issue or question, but if you take the time to read a few, you will soon come to the conclusion that the vast majority are just attempts to 'game' the system. They never seem to say anything of real consequence.

Hopefully we have now demonstrated that Article Marketing is probably something that you do not want to include as part of your online marketing efforts. But is there an alternative? Fortunately there is and it's centred around *being yourself.*

Why? Because you cannot be faked! Whereas many articles

were 'written' or produced by people who weren't even involved in the industry that they 'wrote' about, as a business owner you have a vested interest in ensuring that your online reputation matters.

So, whilst you were being muscled out by people who knew how to game the system, the playing field has now been levelled for genuine business owners, such as yourself, as we shall now explain.

Guest Blogging

We will be looking at blogging in more depth in the next section, but for now we would like to introduce a way which allows you to get your content out to a receptive, friendly and interested audience as well as ensuring that you keep Google happy.

Guest blogging is a great way for you to share your content via non competing blogs. All this means is there are loads of websites out there in your local community or in related markets and niches that will welcome your insight and expertise.

These blogs will have an active audience who will match the profile of your customers. Guest blogging allows you to introduce yourself to them in an informal manner.

We will be the first to admit that it is not as easy as article marketing, but that is part of its appeal. It is precisely because of this that it is more attractive.

Whereas before anyone could pitch up on article directories as an 'expert', guest blogging requires a degree of vetting on the part of the blog owner.

Effectively guest blogging is a good way to sort the wheat from the chaff. As an expert in your field you have no need to be concerned with trying to compete against people whose sole motivation is to try to attract traffic by tricking people into believing that they have something worthwhile to offer.

Guest blogging allows you to rise above the fray.

To help you get started, we have a few points for you to consider.

They're out there somewhere!

OK, so you understand the merits of guest blogging, but where do you start? Are there really people that will allow you to post content on their websites? You bet there are - you just have to look for them.

In the next section on blogging we will see that Google loves websites that grow and have plenty of audience participation. Bloggers understand this and as long as you are credible and have something of interest to say then there is every chance that you will find some blogs that would welcome your content.

If you are a local business then you will be pleasantly surprised to learn that there are probably dozens of active local blogs on a wide range of local interest topics. Not all of them will be 'on theme' in terms of your content, but local interest blogs can be a great place to introduce yourself to a local audience.

Some will even invite Guest Blogs so half the battle is won. Just do a quick search in Google for "Guest Blog" followed by your area, town, county, region, as well as searching on your market, industry, niche, etc.. You'll be surprised at what you find. Also search on your keywords followed by "guest blog" or "guest post" or "submit a guest post", etc.. When you get to a blog that you feel may be of interest then look for their guest blogging submission guidelines to help you.

Also look for blogs in your industry that are not competing with you. Maybe your suppliers have a blog and would welcome your input as someone familiar with their products. Ask your Accountant - they will usually have customers from a wide range of different industries, sectors etc. and they may be happy to allow you to share your expertise with the wider community.

Maybe you are a member of a networking group or you know several local businesses that you work with. If they have a blog then why not suggest to them that they allow a guest blog from you. Who knows, maybe you can help them set up their blog and offer some internet marketing advice to them!

Don't focus solely on Page Rank

Previously, Competitive Link Building was all about the Page Rank (PR) and more to the point, getting links from high PR websites (see the section on keywords for more on PR). With guest blogging you are as concerned with connecting with an audience as you are with getting a boost from a page with a good PR.

The fact is that many blogs and their blog posts are not going to attract a high Page Rank in the early days. However, if the blog is active and growing your blog post could have a very long 'half-life' and deliver good qualified traffic for many weeks, months or years ahead.

Look for relationships not links

Whereas article marketing is solely about gaining links, guest blogging is more a question of creating meaningful *relationships*. This is not just with the blog owner, but also with their community.

This is why the choice of blog to post on is much more important than the Page Rank. It could be that you have the opportunity here to interact with your target audience as opposed to just going for the big home run in terms of PR and linking.

The other point here is that guest blogging is almost like your social media calling card. You are politely announcing yourself to a new audience. Hopefully they will want to find out more about you and your website and your blog (supported by your social media profiles) are the perfect way for you to develop a relationship with this audience.

Whereas link building in the old style is purely focused on 'getting the link', guest blogging offers a much more human, natural approach. Every time you guest blog, you can treat this as an opportunity to socialise and get to know the blog owner. In turn this may open new doors to you as they introduce you to their friends and online followers.

Guest Blogging etiquette - forget being online

To get us started let's go back to basics. Let's say that you attend a local networking breakfast group and you are listening to a guest speaker who you find very interesting. They represent an organization with many thousands of customers similar in profile to the types of customers that you have.

This could be a great opportunity for you. You think to yourself that maybe they would be interested in promoting your products and services since they complement theirs perfectly.

What is your next move?

Take 1

You make a bee line for them as soon as they finish speaking. You introduce yourself, thrust your business card in their hand, give them your best sales pitch and ask them straight away whether they would care to introduce you to their customers.

How would they react? Let's be honest. You've just missed that opportunity.

So let's rewind and play that again…

Take 2

Once they have finished speaking you bide your time. You take note of who they're socialising with. Maybe you recognise one or two faces. You spend some time chatting to their colleagues and associates. You mention that you found their colleague's speech very inspiring and you ask for an introduction.

Happy to oblige, they introduce you. You find some common ground and you enjoy a relaxing chat. You explore the issues that were discussed earlier and you take time to demonstrate that you have a genuine interest in the topics they covered.

The conversation moves on and you discuss areas of mutual interest. Naturally they ask what you do and you explain your role and your business.

They can see that you're a credible and knowledgeable person involved in similar markets. Time moves on and you exchange business cards and you both agree to stay in touch.

Over the course of the next few weeks you exchange emails and you hook up via various social media platforms.

You make sure that you keep them up to date on some interesting developments in the market and some reports and white papers that you are confident they will find of interest.

Over time you gain their trust. They are confident that any introductions they make to their customers will be handled with professionalism and discretion. Accordingly they begin to make these introductions on your behalf.

Which of these approaches would you prefer?

It's exactly the same online. If you overlook the basic offline social norms then you are setting yourself up to fail online.

So, rather than just coldly approaching someone or sending broadcasting emails along the lines of "Hi, I love your blog, can I write a guest blog", try to introduce yourself informally. Social media or participating in the comments section of their blog are both perfectly legitimate ways to appear on someone's radar.

Of course, if they make it clear on their website that they do welcome guest posts on relevant themes, then by all means, you should initiate contact. The key point is to do your homework and be prepared to cultivate your relationships.

This is not a sales pitch

By now you will have grasped that guest blogging is an informal, but effective way to be introduced to a warm audience as well as a way to get links to your site.

So, once you have made contact and you have established yourself as somebody credible and with something to say, there are one or two things that you need to bear in mind, the first one being; *this is not a sales pitch.*

If your post is a blatant piece of self-promotion, then your blog host is not likely to take too favourably to their blog being used as an advertising platform. Remember to consider your audience and to aim to inform rather than to sell. If people are interested they will check you out.

Be sure to take the time to check the blog owner's previous content and any other guest posts. You need to determine the point of view of the blog and the audience. If your blog post is diametrically opposed to the prevalent opinions expressed by the blog owner or their community, then it is unlikely that you will get published.

Remember, you must respect the norms and the opinions of your audience rather than antagonising, patronising or hitting them with a hard sell.

100% Original Content Only

OK, you have come this far. You have spent time getting to know the blog owner and you understand their audience.

You have the perfect blog post for them. You have already used this one on a previous blog post you did and it went down a storm. You just dust it off and send it over. Couldn't be easier!

Big mistake!

It may have taken a while to get to know your contact and to analyse their content. The last thing you should do is to blow it all by offering them *duplicate content.* That is, content that you have *used before.*

To ensure the integrity of the blog you must only submit *100% original content* which has been crafted especially for them and their audience.

There are two reasons for this. Firstly, Google does not want to see duplicate content. It prefers fresh new content information which it can present in its search results pages.

Secondly, as you have taken time to take into account your audience, you need to ensure that you write it specifically for them rather than just using a one size fits all approach.

Become a Regular Contributor

Remember that your content is valuable. You are an expert and you have taken time to create something of value.

Usually most of us, if pushed, could condense our knowledge

of a particular issue or question down to a reasonable length. However, we would find it pretty much impossible to fit everything we know about our area of expertise into one short blog post.

It could be a much more effective approach to offer several blog posts which will help their readers to get a greater insight into your area of expertise. If possible, try to avoid firing all of your arrows at once. If the blog owner and their audience value what you have to say then you could offer to become a regular contributor.

Maybe you could be the person that they turn to for expert analysis on developing trends or a perspective on the latest industry news.

Don't forget the Links!

Once you get the hang of guest blogging it could be easily overlooked that you do need to get links back to your website.

Each blog owner will have their own rules regarding links, but they generally understand that the quid pro quo for your time and effort is a *link back to your website.*

Generally this will be in the bio or in the 'About the Author' section (a space at the end of the post where you include some information about yourself) of the blog post.

Check previous guest posts to see if you can determine the blog owner's policy. Do they allow links from within the main body of your post or is it just in the bio/author section? If in doubt, ask the owner for the ground rules, so that you understand them from the outset.

Paid Guest Blogging

One final point before we move on to your own blog, is that you may find from time to time some blog owners will request payment for inclusion as a guest blogger. In a way, this is proof that the SEO arms race is still in progress.

Whereas blatant paid links have become discredited in the eyes of Google, paid guest blogging is how some of the SEO community have adapted to the new rules. Instead of your link appearing on their site with no apparent value in return, it's in fact a more surreptitious use of *paid links*. You pay them in return for what 'appears' to be a genuine exchange of value, i.e. your valuable content for their blog readers, but in fact it's really paid linking in disguise!

So the dilemma that you may face is whether to proceed or not.

There is no easy answer unfortunately. All we can recommend is that you consider whether the blog owner is more concerned with turning in a fast buck, than they are in offering their readership *quality* content.

If they're genuinely concerned with their audience, then why would they even consider offering 'off message' content or even content which has been provided by people with whom they have no relationship except that they have been paid to provide a link in return?

It all comes down to the quality of their blog. Things to look out for are the quality of recent posts and the amount of genuine interaction from their audience. Check the comments sections, and visit the websites of the people commenting (if you can).

If in doubt, you may be advised to move on. There will be plenty more opportunities for you, especially as you become a great blogger in your own right.

Speaking of which, that's our next subject. Before that, let's hear Dave's opinion…

Dave's view on Link Building
You know a funny thing has started to happen. Dave is definitely getting more phone calls and people are saying that they have found the website in a Google search. Dave is in sales after all and maybe if he can earn some 'easy commission' then he's not going to say no. He's starting to think that maybe there is something in this internet thing after all.

If only he knew what your next trick is going to be - your brand new company Blog.

Before we get that set up, let's review your link building actions.

Action Plan

1. Submit to some good quality Directories over a period of several weeks.
2. Consider some paid directories and submit to them if you have the budget for this.
3. Submit your website to DMOZ, taking care to follow their guidelines.

4. Identify and submit to local and niche directories.
5. Get listed in Google Places and get reviews from happy customers.
6. Check where your competitors are getting links from. Review each link and ask yourself if the linking sites are Related, Reputable and Regional. Avoid any that do not fit your criteria and pursue those that do.
7. Search for potential guest blogging opportunities. Avoid charging in like a bull in a china shop. Take your time to build relationships by commenting on their blog and via social media.
8. Create 100% original content which takes account of the guest blog's audience. Avoid the hard sell and aim to become a regular contributor if the opportunity arises.
9. Don't forget the anchor text and try to mix it up and attempt to deep link rather than always focusing on links to your home page.
10. Have another cup of tea (or coffee); you've definitely earned it now!

Getting Started with Blogging

Have you noticed that these days, everyone is talking about Blogging? There are Blogs on literally any subject that you can think of.

But why has Blogging become so popular, and what does it mean to you and your online presence? More importantly, how can you use the power of Blogging to benefit your business?

JARGON BUSTER: *What is a Blog? A Blog is basically just a dynamic website or section of your website which lets you add fresh content on a regular basis, and it is important to understand the distinction between a regular website and a Blog. Your regular website tells the world about you, your business, your products and services. Maybe you have an online catalogue to sell your products. That is the 'business end' of your website.*

Why Your Blog should be different

Your Blog is an opportunity for you to engage with customers and potential customers in a more informal way. Since you can update it whenever you want, it allows you to express yourself more freely than would be the case with the catalogue part of your website. There are not so many constraints, and you have the room to develop ideas and explore new areas.

The bottom line is, that a Blog should be a central part of your Internet marketing strategy.

And here's why...

1. *Search Engines Love Blogs.*
   They love the fact that you are adding new and interesting content on a regular basis. Follow the steps that we will show you, and you will be rewarded in terms of your search ranking.
2. *Blogs Attract Links.*
   Secondly, Blogs are a fantastic way to get links to your website. When someone sees an interesting Blog post, the chances are they will either link back to you, follow you, bookmark you or subscribe to your blog.
3. *Visitors Love Blogs.*
   Thirdly, your visitors will love your Blog, if you can present them with regular and useful content. It helps them get to know you, before they make any commitment to buy your products or use your services.
4. *Blogging and Social Media are a Perfect Match.*
   Finally, Blogging and Social Media tools like Facebook and Twitter, go hand in hand. Increasingly these are the drivers behind online success, so it makes sense to be a part of it.

Blogging is EASY!

Do you know what the really great thing is about Blogging? Building and maintaining a Blog is really easy. Blogging tools allow you to update easily through a content management system, similar to your word processing software.

So if you can browse, you can Blog!

Blogging is Cheap

The most popular Blogging tool is called WordPress, and many hosting companies will offer this for free with their hosting plans. It is extremely easy to set up, customise and manage.

Why Search Engines Love Blogs

Before you run headlong into Blogging, let's just take some time out to consider the points we have covered, and to understand why search engines in particular, love them.

When we looked at Link Building, one of the key themes we learned was that link building is one of the single most important factors behind your search engine position. Remember, a link is like a vote in a popularity contest or an election. Other websites are basically voting for you when they link to your website.

On that basis, if you have a static website which is never updated, how likely is it other sites will link to you? Well, very few usually. OK, if you have invented the next big thing, then maybe it is easy for you to get links. But even then, your competitors will more than likely catch up with you at some point, so you need a way to stay ahead of the pack.

This is where Blogging comes into its own, as a way of building high quality links to your website. On the Internet, 'Content is King', and that is exactly what Blogging offers you. It is a way for you to create engaging and interesting content for your readers. Over time, if you provide useful and informative content, then you can expect that links to your interesting Blog Posts will start to crop up across the Internet.

Useful Tip: Search engines will come back time and again to review your content, and as your Blog grows, you can cross reference posts and other links in your website, which all helps to push you up the rankings. Why not subscribe to our blog and see how we use blogging in our business, (as well as getting access to our latest hints and tips to grow *your buisness*) at www.pickaweb.co.uk/blog/

Getting Your Blog Started

When we mention that they need to start a Blog to people, their reaction tends to be one of the following:

- ✓ I am not a writer
- ✓ I have nothing worth writing about
- ✓ I do not have the time to do this

Let's address these one-by-one, to show you that anybody can create a Blog.

I am Not a Writer

Believe it or not you are a writer! Just a quick look through the 'Sent Items' of your email will probably throw up several dozen Blog posts for you. Look at the responses you send to people when they enquire about your products or services. Your 'Frequently Asked Questions' really are a brilliant place to start.

If you cannot find too many of those, then why not imagine that you are explaining what you do to somebody that has never heard of you or your company before? Better still, someone who has never heard of the product or service that you offer. If it helps, actually picture someone that you know like this in your mind. It could be a brother or sister, a parent or even an auntie or uncle. The reason that this works is that it forces you to break things down into small, understandable chunks of information that this person will understand.

As you perform this exercise, write each one down and this will be the basis for some really informative Blog Posts.

The really great thing about this is that every time somebody asks you something new, you can create a new Blog Post specifically to answer that question.

What's more, in the future you can just refer people to your Blog Posts when you answer their questions. Hopefully they will stay around to learn a little more about you on your Blog.

I Have Nothing Worth Writing About

Are you sure? Have a look out there, because your competitors definitely have.

This provides you with a brilliant opportunity. Just go to Google and type in your industry or market name (e.g. printing company) followed by 'Blog'.

You now have a list of Blogs in your market place. Go to each of them in turn, and check out their last dozen or so Blog posts. Make a note of the subject of these Blog posts. After looking at a dozen or so Blogs, you will have a list of over 100 ideas.

OK, some of them may not be suitable for you, and you certainly do not want to copy other people, but there is nothing wrong with getting inspiration or ideas from your peers or competitors.

Also, check out your supplier's Blogs. See what they are writing about.

Another great idea is the news round up. Remember setting up Google Alerts? Now you have a whole load of content that has been sent to you, ready for summarising into a weekly round-up of topical news.

Also, why not subscribe to any really popular Blogs that you find, using the email sign up or RSS reader, and that way you will get notified immediately when something new is posted.

I Don't Have the Time to do This

Unfortunately, we cannot create more time for you. What we can do though is to offer you a way of making better use of your time when it comes to Blogging.

Before we do that, we need to impress upon you that Blogging and Social Media really are two of the most important ways for you to market your business. What could be more important than that? The bottom line is, that you need to include Blogging as part of your routine.

That said, probably the best thing to do is to keep a note of what it is that you want to Blog about, and set aside a time to write a certain number of posts. If you do this once a month, and you want to post weekly, then just write four posts.

Once you have your posts, login to WordPress and upload them, but rather than publishing immediately, use the 'Schedule' feature, and set the date and time to auto-publish so that you can set it and forget it.

Blog Set Up

When it comes to choosing a Blogging Platform, we would definitely recommend WordPress. It is just the range of plugins available for WordPress means that it offers a high degree of customisation.

You can find out more at the official WordPress website at http://wordpress.org

WordPress is also very popular among designers and developers, so if you do need any assistance, you will not have any problems finding help at a reasonable cost.

Cpanel and Fantastico / Softaculous

If your web hosting company offers Linux Hosting with CPanel, then usually they will have WordPress ready to auto-install, via a tool called Fantastico or Softaculous.

It is extremely easy to install a WordPress Blog. The only thing you need to bear in mind is where you want the Blog to be installed.

We have prepared a set of WordPress videos to help you with this and these can be found by simply clicking on the Resources link at www.pickaweb.co.uk/lazywebsitesyndrome

If you want it to be your full website, then you need to select the option 'Install on domain' - be aware that if you do this, and you have a website already, then this will overwrite it!

If you already have a website and you just want to install

your Blog as a section called 'Blog' then you need to select the option 'Install in Directory' and in the space provided enter 'blog'. In this case, your Blog would appear at http://www.yourwebsite.com/blog

If in doubt - ask your web host's support team to assist you.

Dave's View on Blogging

It does seem that Dave is starting to see the light. He has earned some great extra commissions lately so he feels like he's on a winning streak. The only problem is that he is spending a lot of time repeating himself to new customers which means that he is losing valuable sales time.

But now that he understands the value of a blog he uploads all of his Frequently Asked Questions to the blog so that he can point people there to save himself some time.

But this is just the start. Blogging and Social Media are a match made in heaven, so next we'll look at how you can use Social Media for your business.

Action Plan

1. Set up a Company Blog on your website. Make it similar in appearance to your website with a clear link back to the main site.
2. Go through your email sent items to look for examples of Frequently Asked Questions that could be used as Blog Posts.

3. Imagine that you are explaining your products or services to someone who does not understand what you offer. Make notes on every detail or explanation. Use these to create as many Blog Posts as you can.
4. Go to Google and search for 'Your Industry' followed by 'Blog', e.g. 'Printing Company Blog'. Then go through each of the Blogs, and make a note of the subjects of their last dozen Blog entries. Get at least 100 written down, and then use these as inspiration for your Blog.
5. Set up a Blog.
6. Schedule your first months' worth of Blog posts.
7. Check our recommended plugins by clicking on the Resources link at: www.pickaweb.co.uk/lazywebsitesyndrome to make your Blogging effort more effective.

Let´s Get Social!

Some people will tell you that Social Media is the next big thing. Others will say it already is the big thing. Others say it is just a flash in the pan.

So what does Social Media mean for you and your business?

We are not going to pull any punches here.

Failure to understand Social Media and develop a credible Social Media strategy for your business could be the single biggest risk that your business faces.

There, we've said it. Sorry for being blunt but we needed to get that off our chests.

Businesses that fail to 'get' social media need to be prepared to struggle at best in the coming years and in the worst cases to go out of business.

It is as simple and as stark as that.

That is the bad news. We said we wouldn't pull any punches but it is really important that you understand this important point.

But we don't want to dwell on the negatives, so let's move on to the good news!

The good news is that if you have started looking for opportunities to guest blog and if you have set up a blog on your website then you are already well on your way to mastering social media.

Give yourself a pat on the back if you have done either of these. If you haven't and you are still planning this then that is just as important. What is vital though is that you *follow through and implement.*

What is Social Media Exactly?

Let's put Facebook, Twitter, YouTube, LinkedIn and all of the other tools aside for now. Let's go back to basics.

In the section on blogging we stated that:

"Your online reputation matters and this manifests itself in your blog. It is like life. If you care about your reputation then people will come to know and trust you."

This is what Social Media boils down to when you strip away all of the tools and paraphernalia.

Social Media is your ability to attract people to you long enough for them to *know, like* and *trust you.*

If you can achieve this then everything else will fall into place.

Whereas in the old days (we mean the 20th Century), advertising was all about getting the message out from the 'top down' (Buy Our Products!!!), the internet and especially Social Media have turned the tables in favour of us, the consumer.

Nowadays it isn't necessarily who shouts the loudest (e.g.

print advertising, flyers, billboards, cold calling, radio and television adverts), but who engages us best as these will be the companies who *will succeed.*

This is the essence of Social Media. It is sometimes referred to as inbound marketing or *permission marketing.*

If you are not being recommended at some point then your business is at risk.

The companies that 'get' this will succeed at the expense of those that don't.

You see, Social Media is just a range of techniques supported by a set of tools that can dramatically accelerate this process of recommendation (or criticism). Nothing more and nothing less. It is not some kind of magic wand that you can wave over your business.

How can you use Social Media?

Rather than try to convince you of the merits of Social Media, can you answer "yes" to all or any of these statements…

- I would like to be viewed as a go to person in my market or niche.
- I want to be respected by my peers and my customers.
- I want to be able to engage more closely with potential customers and existing customers.
- I want to ensure that my company and my products or services are considered as the first choice in my customers' minds.
- I want to be able to reach new audiences and allow

them to discover more about my business 24*7 and in a format they feel comfortable with.
- I want to find similar minded partners and suppliers and work with them.
- I want people to consider me to be a trusted and valued source of valuable information and insight.
- I would like my existing customers to recommend my company to their network of friends and colleagues.
- I would like to develop a network of contacts who I can work with and develop mutually beneficial relationships.
- I want to row across the Atlantic on a water biscuit!

OK, we put the last one in to check that you are still reading, but can you start to recognise how Social Media can help you to achieve these goals?

Community is the Key

The key to success in Social Media is to create a community or to build an online Network. As with any form of human activity, your ability to network depends on your willingness to build relationships and the willingness of others to reciprocate.

A good analogy is to think of Social Media as being like a cross between a cocktail party, a chamber of commerce and a trade fair! A pretty big one too, it must be said.

Cast your mind back to the section on Guest Blogging. Do you remember the two examples of how to approach somebody at a networking event?

Social Media is the same. It is not the place to try to sell. Your website is more than capable of that. Social Media is your opportunity to politely introduce yourself. Once people start to get to know you they may want to learn more about you. Your blog is the perfect place for them to do this. Once they trust you then you have a relationship.

From now on, if they need you they know where to find you.

What happens next depends on the nature of your business or the relationship. Maybe you have a new customer or maybe you have a new partner and you can start to recommend one another.

The point here is that we need to strip away some of the mystery surrounding Social Media. At its heart it is a tool to help you *connect* and *create a community*.

Stick to the basics and you will be just fine.

Useful Tip: Go to social media sites prepared to be a helpful member of the community. Share your knowledge. Help people, encourage them, laugh with them, and get to know them - just as you do in real life.

Now that you understand the importance of Social Media, let´s show you exactly how you can use this powerful tool to benefit your business.

Establish Your Social Media Profile

Many small to medium sized business know that they need to 'do something' about social media. They see it everywhere.

It is on television, in adverts and everyone seems to be talking about it. There are loads of books and blogs that seem to talk about vague terms like "maximising brand value" or "engaging in a diverse communication with your clients".

This all sounds fine, but what if you are a plumber in Manchester or an accountant in Birmingham? What do all these things really mean and can social media really help your business or is it just a distracting waste of your time?

Before you start, we want you to focus on who you are, what you do and how this helps to define your Social Media Profile.

To achieve this we have created the following Social Media Profiles to help you:

- Local Hero
- Local Hub
- Host
- Coach
- Niche
- Player

We have described these in more detail below:

Local Hero

You are a small local business serving the local community and some business customers. You operate within a 5 to 10 mile radius of your workplace or home. You are usually a Sole Trader or Family Business and will usually be a Limited Company. Examples would be plumber, electrician, gardener, builder, joiner/carpenter, painter, personal financial adviser, personal fitness trainer, roofer, therapist, letting agent / estate agent / real estate management (domestic property), removals and storage (domestic), vehicle repair and maintenance, upholstery, dry cleaning, child care services, dentist, driving school, vet, architects (domestic), party organiser, interior designer, wedding / family photographer, etc..

Local Hub

You provide business products or services to your local community. You do not sell to the public, only business to business. You offer services within a limited geographic area which in some cases can be throughout your county. You are not a national company. Examples would be accountant, administrative / business support services, legal services, printer, cleaning services, web designer, designer, graphic designer, marketing agency, IT Services, Computer Services and repair, engineering, recruitment/employment agency, letting agent / estate agent / real estate management (commercial property), logistics / distribution / delivery, plant and machinery hire, office fitters, agricultural supplies, architects (commercial), corporate hospitality, builders / plumbers merchant, removals and storage (commercial), security services, etc..

Host

You are an independent company with your own premises operating in the hospitality, lifestyle, health, beauty, fitness or entertainment industry. You are not typically part of a franchise although if you are then you are responsible for your own marketing. Your customers tend to be locally based or can be national or international in some cases such as hotels. Your customers are a mix of the general public and business customers. Examples would be an independent hotel, bed and breakfast, café, baker, beauty salon, hairdresser, independent fashion retailer, guest house, tourist attraction, theatre, spa/fitness centre, dance school, art and crafts, restaurant, gastro-pub, etc.

Coach
You are a professional providing coaching or consultation services primarily to businesses and in some cases individuals. You are mobile and you can operate on a local, regional, national and international level if required. You may have several colleagues to support you. Examples would be Corporate Training, Life Coach, Business Mentoring, Leadership, Health and Safety, etc..

Niche
You are a business offering products or services over the internet. You are usually a reseller and do not have a large warehouse or hold a huge amount of stock. You could be selling services that can be electronically delivered. You have an ecommerce website to take online payments. Your customers tend to be nationwide although you can sell to overseas clients. Examples would be IT hardware, online jewellery store, home furnishings, legal documents, software, home and leisure, lifestyle, Business Broker, etc..

Player
You are an individual who has earned the reputation as the 'go-to' person in your industry or market. You are a successful business owner and whilst you are not a household name you may have many hundreds or even thousands of business clients. You may offer physical products, services, digital products, motivational, speaking or consultancy services. Your customers will be spread out across the

country and your reputation is international. You are an author and speaker. People will pay to listen to your opinions.

Establish your Social Media Role

How did you get on? Do you recognise yourself? If you didn´t find an exact match, don't worry too much, just try to see the profile that best describes your situation.

Now that you have your profile, let´s consider your *Social Media Role.* Once we have this we will give you some examples to illustrate how you can use Social Media for your business.

Local Hero Social Media Role
Your Social Media Role is to demonstrate your skill, your knowledge and the high quality of your work. Your aim is to become the 'go-to' person in your community for your particular skill. Central to your success is your ability to generate referrals from satisfied clients.

You will use Social Media to showcase your work, possibly with 'before and after' examples using images or video where appropriate. This will allow you to reach out to the friends and contacts of your customers both past and present.

Your role is to identify similar Local Heroes within your area which will enable you to create a mutually beneficial referral network. The result will be that you represent a Single Point of Contact for your customers because your recommendations are trusted.

You will also aim to build contacts with Local Hubs as these represent your opportunity to access your local business community.

Local Hub Social Media Role

Your Social Media Role is to ensure that you are a central facilitator for your business clients. You will continually offer them high quality and relevant information. You will have a good understanding of their business and as a Local Hub you will use this knowledge to identify opportunities for them and promote them whenever possible.

You will use Social Media to keep your customers up to date on key industry trends and insights. You will also use it as part of an effort to 'ring-fence' your clients by ensuring that you are more than just a supplier. This could be by offering seasonal promotions, offering awards/prizes or by arranging networking events.

You will use Social Media to introduce them to your chosen, trusted partners by means of Joint Venture activities.

In short your Social Media Role is that of a trusted and valued advisor.

Host Social Media Role

As a Host, your Social Media Role is to ensure that your facilities are considered as the destination of choice in your area. You will use social media to ensure that you maintain contact with customers past and present to develop long term relationships with them and to be referred to your customers' network.

You will look to identify appropriate Local Hubs and other

(non-competing) Hosts with the intention of offering incentives, discounts, packages, joint offerings and seasonal offers to your customers.

Your Social Media Role is also to create a Buzz around your business. You will identify local events and attractions and ensure that you feature heavily in these wherever possible.

You will host 'taster' events for Local Hubs to showcase what you have to offer with clearly defined follow up offers for their customers.

In short, your Social Media Role as a Host is to be the destination of choice for your customers.

Coach Social Media Role

As a Coach your Social Media Role is to be your customer´s expert of choice in your chosen field.

You aim to ensure that your customers are up to date and compliant in your field of expertise. As a respected professional you have developed relationships with many complementary, non-competing coaches and you can draw on their expertise when required.

Your Social Media Role will involve offering high quality, free information to your clients and prospects in digital and printed formats. You will be working on or have published a book.

You will also use Social Media to reach out to fellow Coaches to create Joint Venture offerings.

You aim to become a Player within 1 year.

Niche Social Media Role
As a Niche, you are regarded as the supplier of choice by your customers. They value the choice, value for money and convenience that you offer. If they need something from you they expect to be able to locate it, order it and receive it in the shortest possible timeframe.

You will use Social Media to keep in contact with your existing customers and to keep you in mind when they need new products or services. New product releases, demonstrations, comparisons, competitions, seasonal offers and discounts will all be part of your social media role.

Social Media will allow you to get recommendations for your products and services from your customers as they introduce you to their online circle of friends.

You can also engage with them to ask them questions which will help to raise awareness of your brand but also to get vital customer feedback and input.

You can also use Social Media to identify new suppliers, partners and distributors.

Social Media will also give you the opportunity to take part in online discussions regarding your niche so that you can establish yourself as the 'go to' expert on the subject. This will play a vital role in raising your company profile.

Player Social Media Role
As a Player, Social Media will prove to be one of the most

powerful tools available to you. As head of your online community you are a respected individual. Your opinion matters and you have the power to influence the behaviour of your followers.

As well as a 'thought leader' your Social Media Role is to identify and partner with other Players in Joint Venture (JV) activities. Typically this will be to cross promote your products, services or events.

Social Media will also provide your followers with a chance to get the inside track on a wide range of areas whether specific to your area of knowledge or to share some personal moments.

Video will be your primary source of content supported by in depth white papers or e-books.

Social Media at Work – Some Examples

Now that you have established your Social Media Profile and Role we can look at some examples to help you to visualise how you could use Social Media to your advantage.

We should point out that these examples are fictional and are purely to give you a framework to help you create your social media strategy.

Local Hero - Social Media in Action

We would like to introduce you to Richard.

Richard runs a local handyman service. He specialises in plumbing, drainage and heating to householders in his local town. He is courteous and helpful and he has a faithful set of customers who trust him to deliver value for money services. He never overcharges and he is always polite and punctual. If he is delayed for an appointment he always makes a point of calling as soon as possible to avoid keeping his customers waiting.

As well as plumbing related issues, Richard is often asked whether he can help in other areas ranging from electrical issues to painting, guttering and general building work. Knowing that his reputation for excellent service is on the line, Richard has been careful to choose who he recommends.

He has a group of partners who he knows that he can recommend without fear of them delivering anything other than to his own high standards.

His partners, in return provide a steady stream of new customers as they refer their customers to him whenever the occasion arises.

Whilst not being a 'techie' as such, Richard is not blind to the opportunities that the internet can offer him. He has had a basic website for years and recently he started his own blog.

At first he couldn't really find much to write about so he thought that he would just stick to what he knew; plumbing and heating. Basic stuff really but the sort of thing he would do day in day out and which he thought might be useful, such as changing washers, bleeding radiators, cleaning calcium from tubes; that type of thing.

Then he bought himself a smartphone for work and one day

he needed to take a short film of a type of tap fitting that he didn't often encounter. He wanted to show his plumbing merchant the type of tap he was working on. The plumbers merchant was impressed and noted that someone had come in the other day from a neighbouring house and they were having all sorts of problems fixing the exact same issue.

Recognising a friend in need, Richard completed the work and took time to film it with his smartphone. Nothing flash, just a two minute video that he knew would save that person hours of problems.

That night, Richard uploaded his video to YouTube - why not, everybody else seems to. It only took a couple of minutes. He called his video "How to fix a Crosshead Wall Mounted Bath Filler" and underneath it he put a link to his blog.

Just to be on the safe side, he also wrote a few lines in his blog so that people would have some step by step instructions in case they needed any help. He also noticed in his blog tool (WordPress) that there was a little YouTube icon, so he followed the instructions and included the video in his blog post. He published it all and sent a quick email to his friend at the plumber's merchant to show him.

Then a day or so later something curious started to happen. Richard started getting notifications in his email inbox that people were commenting on "How to fix a Crosshead Wall Mounted Bath Filler" on his blog.

"Thanks Richard! You're a star!" - this was from the plumber's merchant's customer.

"Am I glad I found you. You've saved me about 3 days of running around!" that was from someone about 200 miles away.

Over the coming weeks, Richard started to receive them from Australia, Canada, the United States, Spain and a few places in between.

He started to respond to them to say thank you.

Then people started to ask Richard for his Facebook Fan Page and did he have any more videos to share?

Richard pretty quickly got the hang of what he soon learned was called "Social Media", despite considering himself a bit of an 'accidental blogger'.

He created a Facebook Fan page and kept his contacts up to date with his videos and his useful hints and tips. He would answer questions and he created a group dedicated to helping people save money on their household bills.

He continued to make videos with his smart phone on everyday issues he would come across during the course of his work. He also started doing short 'before' and 'after' videos to show how he approached a particular task. He would upload these to his YouTube channel and embed them into his blog posts.

As his blog following grew so did the amount of traffic to his website and he became the most in demand handyman in the area, because he was sat proudly at the top of loads of different searches in the search engines. (Of course he linked his blog to all of his Social Media sites including LinkedIn and Twitter).

Richard displayed his social media links on his website (Facebook, Twitter, Linkedin, YouTube & Google Plus). He also installed a social media feature so that people could share, like and bookmark his content.

Over time he found that he was being approached by local businesses through LinkedIn. They liked what they had seen of him online and they were usually looking for help maintaining their business premises. It hadn't really occurred to Richard to do business services but he soon found that it was a lucrative area to work in.

As the commitments on him grew he realised that he needed help. He used his contacts in LinkedIn to get recommendations for partners to help him serve his needs. He even used it to look for staff as he found that the people he came to know and trust could be relied upon to give him an honest appraisal of a prospective new member of staff or potential partner.

He also found LinkedIn an excellent tool for identifying local business owners and decision makers - the type of people who would be interested in his services.

Of course, as Richard's business grew so did his reputation. Unfortunately things did go wrong from time to time and he was usually the first to find out via Twitter. He loved the way that he could use Twitter as a supercharged listening post so that he could immediately respond to both praise and criticism from his customers.

Local Hub - Social Media in Action

Let's move on to Owen.

Owen is an accountant and he is great at his job. He loves to help his customers grow their business. Whereas most accountants were just focused on 'the numbers' Owen was more interested in the people behind the business.

He knew that as an Accountant, his role was more than just someone who ran payroll and the end of year accounts. Owen was at his best when he was helping struggling business owners turn things around.

Despite this, things were not going as well as Owen would have liked. He seemed to spend forever chasing around for potential customers with little to show for it.

He attended network meetings and all he ever seemed to get was a pile of business cards. His mail shots ended up in the bin and he had spent a small fortune on pay per click adverts with not a lot to show for it.

But what really hurt Owen most, as an accountant, was knowing that he was getting a low return on his marketing spend.

But he knew with certainty that if he could just attract more customers, then they would act as his loyal representatives and they would repay him by referring a constant source of new customers.

The thing is, Owen had plenty of extra capacity in his practice to accommodate many more customers. This was partly due to his use of a really neat online accounting tool provided by a specialist Accounting Software Company.

This tool integrated easily with his customers' bank accounts and billing systems and it meant that tasks such as end of year accounts, profit and loss, balance sheets and the like could be quickly and easily produced.

The only fly in the ointment was getting the customer up to speed so that they could learn how to use the tool. It was pretty easy to use but as with anything there was a bit of a learning curve. A few phone calls to the client usually got them up and running though.

Then one day Owen had a bit of a light bulb moment. He had seen a few videos on YouTube where people captured the content of their PC screen and provided a commentary on what they were doing. They ranged in quality from clearly home made to quite professional. One thing is for sure they didn't look that difficult to make.

After some investigation Owen identified several screen capture tools and settled on a product that cost him around £60 (for our US readers that's about $100). Little did he realise that this would probably be the best £60 he would ever spend.

Owen dusted off the headset and microphone that he had bought along with his PC but never used and he got to work. It took a few attempts to get it right but after a couple of hours he had several short videos with his voiceover.

These videos showed his customers in clear, concise steps, exactly how to set up the online accounting tool and how to integrate it with their billing systems and bank accounts.

The next thing he needed was a way to distribute them. He wanted a way that was easy for his customers to use and which they could access at a time that suited them and which they would always be able to access.

YouTube seemed the perfect way to do this. In fact, one of Owen's clients, Richard the handyman mentioned that he had been having some success with YouTube so Owen gave him a call.

Richard gave him his approach of uploading videos and then embedding them into his blog. Pretty soon Owen's blog had several great posts with videos.

Then a funny thing happened. Owen started to receive a steady stream of comments on his blog and gaining followers on his YouTube channel.

He didn't really know why this was, but what was really strange was that they weren't from his regular customers. In fact it seemed that people from all over the world, who used this particular accounting tool, were getting back to him with thanks.

"Great video! Thanks for sharing. I'd been wondering how to set that up".

"You're a star. My accountant just told me to check the help files which were just gobbledygook to me. You've probably saved me about a day's work each quarter."

These were typical comments he was getting.

Never one to miss an opportunity, Owen started to create more videos. But he didn't limit himself to screen share. He was the type of person who would jump at the chance to get in front of a whiteboard with coloured pens (if he needed to get a particular point across). He had loads of presentations stored on his hard drive, so he thought that maybe he could bring them to life on video.

In fact, one of Owen's clients, Matt was a wedding photographer and videographer. He owed Owen a favour so he thought he'd call it in. He didn't want to take up too much of Matt's time, but he was sure that if he could run him through a few basics about setting up the camera and lighting, he would be able to create his own videos in his office.

Matt was more than happy to help and once Owen had invested in a tripod, a lapel microphone and a couple of lights, he was ready for action.

After some trial and error, Owen had produced a set of videos aimed at helping small businesses manage their finances. Whilst they weren't going to win him any prizes in presentation techniques, they would definitely be of use to his clients and his growing band of followers on his blog and his YouTube channel.

Some people asked Owen how he managed to produce such great looking videos, so Owen thought it would be a great idea if Matt could show how they did it. He didn't want to take credit, when it was Matt who had showed him.

Matt, always happy to oblige, set to work and made a great video which covered the basics of creating a great video on a shoestring budget.

Matt's video appeared on Owen's blog as a 'guest post' and pretty soon Matt started to get calls from people interested in his work.

This got Owen thinking and he figured that maybe his success with YouTube could be another way to help his clients.

So he contacted them all and explained the benefits of guest blogging and asked if they would like to create a blog post for him. A few of them were apprehensive, but after a bit of persuasion they all agreed. Fairly soon, Owen's blog was alive with loads of useful blog posts from his customers.

Since then Owen has become the champion of his customers' interests. He set up a small business Group on LinkedIn and Facebook. Initially for his clients, they soon attracted plenty of outside interest and became really lively, but friendly forums for debate.

In fact, Owen was able to take these Groups offline and he set up quarterly get-together's as well as other informal face-to-face events.

Owen also became an avid fan of Twitter. Whereas before he would have just looked blankly at the screen and wondered what to tweet about, he set up an automated Twitter tool which allowed him to search in real time for mentions of keywords related to his clients business. He was always on the lookout for opportunities for them.

Owen made sure he shared useful content on all of his social media accounts such as Facebook, Twitter, Linkedin, YouTube & Google Plus. He also noticed that when people comment, share, or like (+1) the content he shares it seems to help with his position in the search results as Google takes social factors into account when determining its search results.

He created a Google+ personal profile and a business page. He soon noticed that when he posted his content here that it actually got indexed in the Google search results which meant that he started to get even more traffic from people searching in Google.

He doesn't spend hours and hours using it, but he makes sure that he adds his contacts into Google + circles and interacts with them. This is another great way for him to network online.

The funny thing was that Owen didn't really feel that this was marketing or advertising. He just felt that he was being himself - helpful, friendly and focused on helping his clients to grow their businesses.

But whilst it didn't feel like marketing or advertising, the results could not have been clearer. Over the next year, Owen was looking to grow his business by 100%. In fact, he was starting to look further afield to new towns and he was considering setting up a franchise based on his brand.

Host - Social Media in Action

The next person we'd like to introduce you to, is Emma.

Emma is the owner of a small hotel "The Dovecote Hotel" that she had inherited from her parents and it was as much a labour of love as it was a business. Located several miles outside a popular market town, her typical customers were tourists and the occasional businessperson.

Emma prided herself on her professionalism and eye for detail. Rooms were decorated in a charming country style which relayed a sense of calm without being chintzy. The hotel restaurant was based more on traditional favourites rather than haute cuisine. One thing Emma was a stickler for though, was local produce was used whenever possible.

Tourist business was pretty brisk, especially in the summer months, but the problem was weekday occupancy. What Emma really wanted to do was to establish herself as a choice for business travellers.

She was sure that they would appreciate the homely charms of her hotel. The cozy rooms, the fireplace in the Lounge and the comforting traditional food, based on local ingredients.

The problem was reaching out to the business community. That isn't to say that Emma hadn't tried. Goodness knows how much she had spent on various advertising campaigns, without much to show for it. It just seemed such a hard nut to crack.

It wasn't the location, as the hotel was in easy reach of town and was on one of the main roads .

It wasn't the pricing either, as she kept an eye on the big chains (or she tried to match them as closely as possible.)

Business customers, it seemed, were more interested in having a standardised hotel room and facilities, rather than a more traditional offering such The Dovecote's.

That was until a chance phone call. The caller was Owen, Emma's accountant. It was simply a courtesy call, to see how business was going. That was what Emma really valued about Owen's company. They seemed to take a real interest in what she was up to.

She mentioned in passing that she would really like to get more business customers during the week, as that was her quiet period.

He suggested that Emma sign up for LinkedIn. She had never heard of it, but Owen was kind enough to send her over an email with a link to his blog where he explained in a 5 minute video what LinkedIn is, and how to create an account.

It all sounded interesting and she was curious to learn more. The reason that Owen mentioned LinkedIn was that he knew that her target market was business people and LinkedIn is a networking site for business people.

So far, so good, but Emma was concerned that whilst she was 'in business' and as such she was eligible, all these people seemed to be what she termed 'real business people'. She just wasn't sure she would fit in.

Owen recommended that she join a local LinkedIn Group as

well as any groups she could find that were related to the hospitality industry.

Emma spent some time searching around and eventually found a few Groups to join. Most of them seemed friendly enough. Some of them even asked questions and Emma found that she could actually answer a few of them back. Nothing major, just hints and tips. She had the hospitality industry in her veins and she knew the local area like the back of her hand, so she knew she was a valuable and trusted source of local information.

To her surprise she found that she really enjoyed sharing her knowledge. In fact, it became a bit of a ritual for her and she was always eager to login to her LinkedIn account first thing in the morning, to see if she had any replies.

One day, she found a message sent directly to her LinkedIn account. It was from Hazel Williams who ran her own Corporate Hospitality and Events business. She was based in town and she explained that she had an urgent requirement and could they catch up to see if Emma could help.

Emma was intrigued. Why would this person who runs a 'real' company like this be interested in me? Despite her doubts, she got in contact with Hazel who immediately put her mind at ease.

Hazel explained that she was organising a large conference for a major pharmaceutical company in town. Unfortunately one of the main hotels was overbooked and she was desperately searching around for local hotels to cope with the overflow.

She mentioned that she kept seeing Emma's name crop up in the Question and Answers and she always seemed knowledgeable and helpful so she wondered if she might be able to help.

Then it all started to fall into place. LinkedIn is a great place to meet business people, but rather than trying to sell your services, the idea is to *introduce yourself* and be a *helpful* member of the community. Eventually, if someone needs you, they will find you.

Suddenly all sorts of opportunities started to spring to mind. But that was for the future. For now, Emma had an immediate requirement.

She had to remain focused and keep her eyes on the prize.

As it happens she was able to accommodate Hazel's need with ease. It goes without saying that her new customers were thrilled with the welcome that Emma laid on for them.

From this point on, Emma realised that the key to her success was her ability to make connections online. It was fun once you got the hang of it.

Her approach was simple. She would look to identify where her potential customers would be clustered together. Companies like Hazel's were excellent potential sources of new leads. It made sense that if someone already had customers that fitted her profile then it would be a better use of her time to approach that person, rather than trying to approach them individually.

Emma was quickly learning that *recommendation* is a powerful marketing tool.

She looked for people involved in Corporate Hospitality, Event Management, Training, Human Resources, Recruitment and several other key sectors.

Then Emma decided that she would create her own Group for local businesses. She reasoned that if she was the head of the group, this would then enable her to extend her network far more quickly.

She was right on the money.

Her group quickly established itself as a friendly and welcoming group for local businesses. She was careful to ensure that new members received as warm a welcome as if they were customers at her hotel.

Over time she started to notice that she was being approached by numerous local businesses with requests to partner with them or for help to promote their events. These included themed evenings and cooking schools.

On such occasions she would offer a discounted rate to her partners' customers as they were effectively acting as unpaid salesmen. Her partners in turn were happy, because they knew that their customers would be well cared for.

Emma also started using Facebook and Twitter. She found that these appealed much more to her tourist guests. She used these to create a buzz around her hotel with special offers, news and upcoming events featuring heavily.

Twitter was really useful for joining local interest conversations and for responding really quickly whenever a question or a conversation arose which included any relevant terms. Emma was careful never to promote her own business. She just offered her advice and expertise as a local Hotel owner. This way she appeared on the radar when anyone was asking questions about her area.

Business is good for Emma. She has managed to build up high mid-week occupancy rates thanks to the business customers that she attracts via LinkedIn as well as being the hotel of choice for tourists new to the area.

Coach - Social Media in Action

It had been a long day for Jennifer.

As she stretched out in her cosy room at the Dovecote Hotel she thought about the long journey home that she faced tomorrow.

She had been to see a prospective new client, Stephen Phillips at County Camping for her new Business Coaching company. Having spent a week pulling together a fantastic report on how to grow a business, she was really disappointed to learn that this potential client did not have the time to implement her ideas.

Since leaving her job 6 months previously she found being self-employed far from the liberating experience she had hoped it would be.

In fact, it would be true to say that she was wracked with self-doubt. What had seemed like such a good idea a few months ago, was rapidly turning into a bit of a nightmare.

She couldn't put her finger on what she was doing wrong. Whatever it was, she was not finding enough clients and those she did find, weren't really the right profile she needed to be working with.

She had fantastic presentations, her marketing materials and brochures had been professionally designed and printed. Her reports were hard hitting and well-argued but they just did not seem to be opening the right doors for her.

At least she could console herself with the fact that she was in a lovely hotel and there was the prospect of a delicious meal to look forward to.

As she had to be off first thing in the morning, she came down early for her dinner. The owner, Emma was the only person in the restaurant and they soon started up a conversation.

Jennifer explained that she was down on business and that her meeting hadn't been successful and she soon found herself telling Emma about her disappointments in terms of her new business.

"The most frustrating thing I find" she explained, "is the amount of time I have to put into my reports. This is all pre-sales. I don't get paid for it unless the client accepts my proposals and we start the implementation".

"Then why don't you give them away?" asked Emma casually.

"Sorry, but maybe you don't understand my business" replied Jennifer. "In our game, you are what you know. If I start giving it all away then these are my trade secrets. Would you give away all of your best recipes for example?" she asked.

"No. But I know they'll enjoy the results" laughed Emma.

That got Jennifer thinking. She knew that half of the time most of the people she met just did not have the time or the inclination to implement her findings. To be honest, she often thought it wouldn't matter if she presented them with "The Perfect Report for Your Business". She knew that taking action was the missing ingredient, not so much the content of her reports.

After her meal she headed off for bed & she found that she slept pretty soundly that night, in fact, more soundly than she had for weeks.

When she woke the next morning it felt as if a cloud had been lifted. She couldn't put her finger on it, but she thought back to Emma's words last night and she vowed that, from now on she would, indeed, give them the recipe, as it were.

Jennifer headed home and that week she cranked into action. She cleared her diary and worked feverishly for days to pull together several high impact reports. They were all based on her previous experience gained with a major consulting and accountancy firm and, they were pretty impressive.

The only problem was delivering them. How could she get them in front of an audience that would be interested in them?

It was then that Jennifer remembered one of those little sayings that consultants are so fond of saying: "Don't fire all of your arrows at once".

This gave her an idea. She understood Google well enough to know that it loves content and rewards websites that have loads of content. She also knew that blogging was a great way to attract visitors to your website. She understood that people will often stumble across your website in the search engines if your blog post was set up correctly.

So her strategy would be to break her reports further down into bite-size chunks that she could use as blog posts which she could use as bait for her reports. If people like my blog posts she thought, they'll love my reports.

Thorough as ever, Jennifer performed an analysis of the competition. There were some people that kept cropping up all over the place. She made a note of their names and called these the 'Players'. These Players seemed to be clearing up. Not only did they have their own websites, they also seemed to be appearing on other people's websites too.

The other thing that she noticed was that whenever you went to one of these sites, they were always trying to get your contact details in return for a free report. She tried a couple and found the whole process very straightforward.

You enter your name and email address, in return you got an email asking you to confirm, and once you did, you then had access to the free report. Naturally, her reports were far more compelling, but she had to admit that her competitors' reports were not without merit.

What was really impressive though was that they all remembered her and kept in touch with her by email. How touching. "That must take them ages!"

Then she smelled the coffee. These emails were actually automated and had inserted her name into a pre-written email. Some quick research and she found a system called Aweber which allows novice users to set this up on their website or blog.

She had the nucleus of a strategy. She would break her reports into chunks and post them to her blog. When people come to her blog, she would then offer them a more in depth report in return for their email address and she would then follow up automatically by email.

Her new blog was soon set up and she started to upload posts on a regular basis. She even had it set up so that she could upload her material in advance and set a date for her blog to automatically publish at a pre-determined date.

The problem was that whilst this was all set up, she was not getting sufficient traffic to her blog. It was then that she revisited her analysis of the competition and she looked again at some of her competitors' tactics.

She noticed that many of the Players that she kept seeing, were partnering with other people in the industry. It didn't seem to be that formal an arrangement though. It could sometimes be a post on a blog or a video interview.

In fact, she also noticed that some of the emails she was receiving from one person contained offers to sign up for something offered by one of the other Players.

It all seemed like one big merry-go-round for them. If only she could work out a way to get on board, then she would be able to pick and choose her customers.

She felt apprehensive about contacting a Player because she wouldn't have much to offer in return. But she had noticed that there appeared to be a second rung of people and she made it her mission to start here.

She studied their blogs and she started to comment on them just to get noticed. Sometimes she found that they actually responded to her comments, but other times her comments did not appear.

The interesting thing was she found that doing this kind of work was a great way to get ideas for her own blog, so she kept a note of any ideas she could write about in the future.

As she found more and more blogs though, she found that she was having trouble keeping up and she needed a way to rationalise this process to make sure that she was being as efficient as possible with her time.

Eventually she found a tool that would dramatically improve her ability to keep up: an RSS reader. RSS stands for Really Simple Syndication and an RSS reader is just a tool that allows you to consolidate all of the blogs that you have subscribed to into one place. That way you can see all updates in one place, rather than you having to go and search for them. The best thing is that it is free. Jennifer used the Google Reader for this purpose.

Now Jennifer was really up and running. She was sure that if she could start to appear on the blog comments of these blogs that she could establish herself as a serious contributor.

Jennifer put her plan into action and she patiently started contributing to a select number of blogs. Not the Players' blogs, but the tier of people she had identified below them.

She took time to ensure that her comments were constructive and made a contribution to the conversation. She avoided any form of self-promotion whatsoever but from time to time she would offer some advice too.

She was also careful to avoid criticising anybody in any way, shape or form. She noticed that there were a few negative comments from time to time and they really reflected badly on the person posting. If ever anyone criticised her she would rise above it.

Interestingly enough, whilst she was not seeing a huge increase in traffic, she did start to notice more action on her blog and she started to get people signing up for her free reports. Basically she was 'hanging out' where her target market was to be found.

After a few weeks of concerted effort she noticed that the blog owners started to comment on her comments. Nothing major, and usually it was just a note of thanks.

It was at this point that she felt she could reach out to them. She reasoned that now that they recognised who she was, they would now be more responsive to her. The question was, "how to approach them?"

She looked at their blogs and their profile pages always seemed to lead to a LinkedIn profile. Jennifer had set up a LinkedIn profile ages ago, at her old job but she had never really kept it up to date.

So she updated it, and set about contacting these people. Rather than sending off a template request for contact, she customised it specifically for the reader and wherever possible she made reference to the comments she had left on their blog.

She was pleasantly surprised to learn that most of them responded positively to her and seemed very welcoming. In fact, one or two invited her to post something on their blog. This was what she had been hoping for and soon Jennifer was contributing guest posts to a number of key blogs.

From here she moved on to video interviews and soon she was an established member of the 2nd tier of bloggers. She would interview them from her home office using a webcam, a microphone and Skype. She recorded them using a low cost recording tool and it was so easy she almost felt guilty.

Once she had the interviews, she would get them transcribed for her blog and she had some great new content. She was basically offering to promote these people on her blog in return for some great content. It seemed a very equitable arrangement.

Suddenly people started to notice her and she was getting invited to all sorts of networking events both online and offline.

She also started to get more people signing up for her free reports.

She branched out into using Facebook and pretty soon she had a small community of fans and she created a *Business Growth Club Group* so that she could offer them free advice. She really enjoyed the interaction with these business owners and she felt confident that it was only a matter of time before the work would start to come in.

Jennifer was rapidly becoming a power user of Social Media and it became her principal marketing tool. She soon added Google Plus to her schedule. The main reason for this was that as her content was valuable she wanted to get as much payback as possible. Whilst Google Plus did not have as many people using it as, say Facebook (as it was a newer platform) she loved the way that her content would get indexed in Google which was not the case with other social media tools.

Then one day the phone rang. Even though it had been several months since they last met, she recognised the voice on the other end. It was Stephen Phillips at County Camping and he was wondering if she was interested in working with him after all.

We'll be back for the conclusion of Jennifer's story in a short while, but first we need to spend some time with Stephen.

Niche - Social Media in Action

Since his meeting with Jennifer, Stephen hadn't been able to take things forward as much as he had hoped. Many of

Jennifer's recommendations for his business, 'County Camping', made sense to him, but the truth was that he just didn't have the time to implement them and that is why he declined her offer.

In Stephen's mind that was the justification - *he just didn't have the time.*

Time. It was always a problem. Since starting up his camping website 3 years ago, he never seemed to have enough of it. The business just seemed to consume most of it, and what really got to him was that he wasn't spending as much time with his family as he would have liked.

At first he thought that selling camping equipment online would be great fun. After all, he loved outdoor pursuits, so what could be better than selling stuff that he loved doing himself?

The reality was that what had started out as good fun was suddenly starting to feel like a job. A not a very enjoyable one at that! This was a job where the buck stopped with him. The business seemed to pull him in all sorts of different directions.

Stephen's intentions from the start were to be an online retailer. He had avoided setting up a physical shop because he had previously worked in a camping store and he felt that the internet offered him much more potential for growth. It also meant that he didn't have the initial overhead of physical premises to worry about.

He had built up a range of contacts whilst in the shop and he worked closely with a number of recognised suppliers.

In the early days, growth had been very quick. He seemed to have hit upon a market that was really growing. His website had improved slowly but surely from a fairly basic set up to a pretty slick tool. He had automated as much as possible so that things like creating customers' invoices were all taken care of automatically.

But Stephen had two problems. First was stock and distribution and second was growth. Unfortunately they were both dependent on each other.

Whilst the internet had allowed him to get up and running without the overhead of having a physical shop, he still hadn't been able to overcome the need to hold stock and deliver it. His stock management skills were, he had to admit, rather haphazard.

His garage had become completely full of equipment and he was holding stock with a storage company whose facilities were on the other side of town. This arrangement was proving rather expensive, partly due to the amount of time it took to locate the stock and then send it.

The other problem Stephen was facing was that sales had flattened out. In some ways this was a good thing, anymore business would multiply his stock problems. In his heart though, he knew that 'hoping not to grow' wasn't much of a business strategy.

Increasingly he felt as though he was losing control of the business and he seriously considered throwing in the towel.

It was at this point that he had originally contacted Jennifer.

He had been really impressed by her. Her management credentials could not be faulted and she seemed to take a genuine interest in his situation.

Her report identified two principal areas that he needed to address. Firstly, if he was to grow the business, he needed to sort out the stock issue. In fact, she was quite blunt on this point. She made it clear that failure to address this issue could have serious consequences for his business.

Secondly, she identified the slow-down in growth to his lack of what she called "Channel Partners". This seemed a bit like management speak to him, but effectively what she was saying was that his whole sales approach was focused on the website & in order to grow the business he needed to *find people* and companies who could sell his products for him.

As soon as he had told Jennifer that he could not proceed with her recommendations, he regretted it.

He felt defeated. He knew in his heart that he should have trusted what she recommended, but he just didn't see how he could find the time to implement it.

They had gone their separate ways, although Jennifer was kind enough to have left Stephen a copy of the report with her recommendations. She had also reassured him that he could contact her whenever he wanted, should he have second thoughts.

That was another of Jennifer's little mottos that she had learned from experience: "Never close a door."

In the meantime, Stephen had continued to limp along until the point where he just couldn't see any way forward. He thought that if he didn't do something soon then the business would just overwhelm him.

It was at that point that he decided to contact Jennifer. He dusted off the report and went straight to her website to get her contact details.

He was pretty impressed with her website. She was offering loads of really useful information. In fact, it had a number of free reports to download. Intrigued he found a few titles that interested him and signed up for them.

Hesitant about phoning Jennifer, he took the time to read the reports in advance so that at least he would have something to talk about. What he was concerned about was the loss of face. He felt as if he was going back to her with his tail between his legs. If he was honest, he just felt a bit of a loser and he was worried that she would just tell him that he had missed his opportunity.

He was pleasantly surprised to receive an email from Jennifer the next day. In fact, not only did she email him directly, she thanked him for downloading the reports and said she would love to discuss his business and she was available if he wanted to chat through anything. She even gave her mobile number.

In fact the email was an automatic 'follow up' (as we shall explain shortly), but to Stephen, it was a lifeline.

He summoned up the courage and called her.

Stephen was quickly reassured that she was not only pleased to hear from him, but he detected in her voice a sense of real excitement about his project. He was just so used to ploughing a lonely furrow that it felt as if a great weight had been lifted from his shoulders.

Over the coming days, they exchanged several emails and held a number of phone calls. In the time between their last meeting Jennifer had certainly not let the grass grow beneath her feet.

She seemed energised and her enthusiasm started to rub off on him.

After several days, she presented him with her recommendations and whilst they hadn't changed in general terms, she had put some meat on the bones of how to implement them.

Her plan was set out in three parts: 1) Identify fulfilment, storage and despatch partners, 2) identify Channel Partners and 3) establish yourself as an 'Authority Figure'.

The surprising aspect was that her approach seemed to be built very much around the use of social media. Stephen had dabbled with Facebook and he could see how that might be used, but Twitter was just a mystery to him and he hadn't even heard of LinkedIn.

Jennifer took time to send Stephen a number of links to blog posts, videos and reports on her website so that he could get up to speed on all of these different tools.

He could see that in terms of identifying suppliers such as the stock and warehousing partner, LinkedIn would be a great way to find people in the industry who could help him. It was clear Jennifer wasn't going to do all of the work for him - that was up to him - but she was just lighting the way for him.

Within just a few days, Stephen had connected with half a dozen potential partners through LinkedIn. They were a mine of information and before long he was familiar with all of the terminology that they used. He actually quite enjoyed learning something new.

At the same time, Jennifer recommended that Stephen should try to identify non-competing niche partners. What she meant by that was Stephen should try to identify companies who have customers that would match his target market. He could then look to set up a partnership arrangement with them. It could be as formal or informal as they like.

For example, some of them may wish to sign up as an affiliate. His website software has an affiliate system built into it and it is really easy for them to earn an affiliate commission. Others may prefer to send an email with a seasonal promotion to their email list of customers. Some may prefer direct mail.

Her strategy was for Stephen to check in Google for any blogs relating to these non-competing niches and to start to comment on them. She advised him to stick to being helpful - this is not a sales opportunity. Initially his aim was to become known to a new audience.

This proved to be a rich seam to mine for Stephen. He was

very pleasantly surprised to learn that there was potentially a huge number of different clubs, associations as well as traditional retailers who were happy to partner with him.

After several weeks Stephen found that the blog owners themselves were initiating contact with him. What was really exciting was they all shared a common interest in all things outdoors, whether it be cycling, adventure holidays or even going to festivals.

Within a couple of months he had over 20 partners promoting his products to their customers.

Fairly quickly it became evident to Stephen that 'social media' is something that he was pretty good at. After all, the only thing that he had to do was to share his knowledge.

Based on his experience, he built up a profile of several partner types. The advantage of this was that when he contacted a prospective partner he could present them with the options available and they could hit the deck running.

At the top of his profiles were (what Jennifer referred to as) 'Strategic Partners'. These were partners with a sizeable database of paying customers. She advised Stephen that these partners would be one of the most important ways to quickly grow his business.

She also introduced him to the concept of Joint Ventures (or JVs) where you identify a common interest with a partner who has a similar sized database to you so that you can cross promote each other's products.

Stephen had thought that 'Strategic Partners', and 'Joint Ventures' were something that only 'real' businesses did (like banks, or airlines) not someone like him! The strange thing was that after a while, it all felt quite natural to implement.

Stephen actually noticed that once he had started to establish his reputation online it became a lot easier to form JVs. In fact on several occasions, potential JV partners actually *contacted him* through LinkedIn.

Another recommendation from Jennifer was to keep a note of any questions that he answered as these would form content of the third part of his strategy: to establish himself as a 'go to' person in his niche.

To do this Jennifer recommended that he needed a vibrant and growing blog supported by videos and free reports for download. This must be supported by an active use of Facebook and Twitter, to ensure that he could address his target market on their territory.

Again, Stephen took to this like a duck to water. He never considered himself a natural salesman, but this was something altogether more enjoyable.

He soon established himself as a committed blogger, uploading content on a wide range of outdoor activities. As well as guest blogging on other people's blogs, he would invite potential partners to post on his. He explained the mutual benefit to them and he would carefully vet who he invited to ensure the integrity of his content. As well as getting great content he found this to be a great technique to build trust with potential and existing partners.

As his subject matter was the great outdoors, Stephen was not short of video opportunities. He kept his smartphone handy at all times and he became very adept at creating quick and informative videos which he uploaded to YouTube and embedded into his blog posts.

As his blog grew in popularity, so did his use of Facebook and Twitter. He soon built up a faithful following on both. In Facebook he created several groups to cater for the different outdoor lifestyle interest groups. These are vibrant, lively forums where the members share their experiences.

As the head of each group, Stephen's role is to extend a warm welcome to anyone interested in outdoor pursuits. They can ask questions or get advice and there is always someone on hand to help.

Using an automated tool, Stephen finally got to grips with Twitter. He loves the way it enables him to not only connect with people who share his passion for outdoor pursuits, but also to keep an ear to the ground for emerging trends and new ideas.

It also enables him to listen to the chatter in real time and to join in whenever he sees a conversation that he can add his experience to. It is a great way for him to introduce himself, although as always, he is careful to avoid promoting his services.

Following Jennifer's advice Stephen also got the hang of Google Plus. She explained that content posted to Google Plus would get indexed by Google. He quickly saw the advantage that this offered him in terms of appearing prominently in the Google search results pages.

It took just a few short months to get there, but in the time that Stephen has been working with Jennifer, he has transformed his business.

Having made a number of contacts via LinkedIn in the warehousing and distribution field, Stephen worked with Jennifer to identify the criteria for a partner and focused on several potential partners. Stephen's stock problem has now been resolved, ensuring that he has more time to focus on marketing his business better.

Stephen also learned that he can use social media to create a buzz around his brand. By committing to his own blog and to contributing to others, Stephen has been able to identify not only partners willing to promote his products but also to draw a new audience to his company. He reinforces this via Facebook, YouTube and Twitter and uses these platforms to keep them involved, informed and up to date on the world of outdoor pursuits.

Stephen and Jennifer stayed in touch and he became something of a poster boy for her services. He provided a video testimonial for her and he was always recommending people to her business.

In fact, Jennifer had asked Stephen to attend a marketing event so that he could talk to the audience about his experiences.

Let's see how he got on…

Player - Social Media In Action

Stephen was pretty shocked when he entered the room. Jennifer had warned him that there would be at least 250 people attending her first two day *Small Business Accelerated Growth Event* but it looked to him as if there were at least double that present.

The room was huge and at the front on a low stage was Jennifer beaming as she welcomed Stephen up to speak.

Undaunted he strode up to the stage. In actual fact, it wasn't half as bad as he had thought it would be. They had rehearsed the questions and they both new his story so well that it appeared natural and unscripted.

Stephen actually found that he was enjoying himself. It was a bit like his business - he was just helping people. It all felt very natural.

But how had Jennifer come so far in such a short space of time? He was sure that when they had first met a little over 2 years ago, Jennifer was just starting out.

Later that evening, during Jennifer's 'Inner Circle' dinner, she explained how she had got there.

She explained that after their first meeting, when he had decided not to proceed, her business only really started to take off once she had immersed herself in social media.

She explained that she initially started to use her social media profiles to lead people to her blog and her free reports to attract and convert people. She then started building relationships with a number of well-known bloggers, mainly by guest blogging and video interviews.

By the time that she had finished working on Stephen's business she had reached the point where she had started to turn potential customers away. For her, that was a bit of a sore point, especially considering where she was just a few months before that; alone and with no business coming in.

That proved a turning point, she explained. She knew from personal experience that it can be lonely out there as a business owner and she was convinced that she could help any business turn itself around.

The best way for her to reach a large audience, in as short a space of time as possible, was to write a book. Her reasoning was that authors are viewed as experts and this fact alone meant that a book could open many doors for her.

After all, she has loads of content from her blog and her reports. She could basically re-use this and give it a context and she would have enough for a book.

But how will she get it published? Who would be interested? It would probably cost a fortune or at the very least involve loads of rejection from publishers.

Undaunted, Jennifer went to work in Google to start her research. She soon found that it is possible to self-publish and that there are people out there who will help and coach you to do this.

From here Jennifer used LinkedIn to find several writing coaches and soon settled on a coach that she felt comfortable working with. The writing process itself was pretty straightforward and the coach took care of getting the book printed and available for purchase from Amazon.

She set to work promoting her book via her online network and pretty soon she found that she was being interviewed on a regular basis by people interested in her thoughts and ideas. If she was honest, she hadn't written the book with any intention other than to get her opinions and ideas out there. However, it soon dawned on Jennifer that her book could be the starting point of a much bigger plan to allow her to help many thousands of business owners.

At first her intention was to use her book to attract potential customers to a seminar event of typically 2 to 3 hours. They were interactive events for up to 15 attendees who all received copies of her book as a gift for attending. Most importantly they got to meet Jennifer in person and many of them found that just being able to speak to someone about their experiences was a real help.

She aimed to run at least 2 or 3 seminars a month but she found that she was getting more and more requests and she started to increase the number. Eventually she was running 2 or 3 a week!

The reason for the increase in her popularity was clear. What she was advocating was easy to understand and follow. She had attracted a faithful following of 'raving fans' who were eagerly recommending her to their friends and associates.

Her live events were also backed up by loads of useful, free content via her website.

At this point Jennifer faced two issues. First was the workload. It was at this point that Jennifer had to decide whether she could keep up such a hectic pace. It was starting to take its toll and she noticed that her presentational style was becoming a little tired and rehearsed.

It wasn't that she was losing interest. On the contrary, she was full of ideas. It was just that the schedule had become so hectic that she was concerned that she was burning herself out.

Secondly, whilst she was getting plenty of great reviews and faithful followers she was not converting this into extra business.

She needed a strategy that allowed her to focus more on conversions and growing her business but not at the expense of the quality of her work.

Again, she performed a competitive analysis but this time focused more on the approach of the Players that she had previously identified. She noticed that they all seemed to have a couple of large events each year, supplemented by membership sites and various Joint Ventures with other Players. They also had a wide array of physical products such as boxed DVD sets, newsletters and other info products.

She decided that now was her time to step up. She had a list of several thousand loyal subscribers so she felt confident that she would be able to create some fantastic products and services to cater for all budgets.

The Small Business Accelerated Growth Seminar was her first major live event. She managed to attract almost 300 people and each attendee had paid several hundred pounds to attend.

She hired a professional videographer to film the event and she produced a DVD box set which she would be able to market from time to time to her list and her JV partners' lists.

She also created a monthly membership website with different levels of membership with loads of great content and features for her clients.

Jennifer continued to offer one to one coaching, but she was able to pick and choose her clients carefully. Of course her services were not cheap, but she could demonstrate that they represented extremely good value for money.

These days Social Media is Jennifer's main source of marketing. Her LinkedIn and Facebook groups allow her both to communicate and to listen. They give her an insight into the challenges and opportunities that her customers face. This enables her to identify new ideas for content and for products and services.

She is a power user in terms of video and YouTube in particular. This enables her to reach a new audience who will often then visit her website and blog to learn more.

But her videos are not just information. She uses them for informal "what I'm doing today" type videos and these help to create a more informal feel for her followers.

Of course Joint Ventures play a vital role in her approach and she finds LinkedIn extremely useful to make connections and identify new partners. In fact she has started to work more and more with overseas Partners especially in the United States where there she sees huge potential for her business model.

Create Your Social Media Plan

Hopefully by now you have seen a common thread in our examples. Did you notice that none of our heroes actually started out with the intention of using social media to grow their business. It is almost as if they fell into it by accident. They mastered social media without actually meaning to.

The advantage that you have is that you do not need to leave it to chance! You can plan it, step by step.

The important point is that you must not to 'force it'. Just be natural and be a helpful member of the community. A good place to start is blogging. Remember that your Blog is the centre of your online Universe. Share your knowledge and ideas through your blog and people will gravitate towards you.

However, before even starting your own, follow Jennifer's example and check out your industry blogs. Make a note of who is blogging, what they write about and what types of media they use.

Make a note of content ideas and where appropriate sign up for reports. If you start to find blogs you really like, subscribe to them and keep up to date by using Google Reader.

Also look for non-competing blogs and blogs related to your market or niche. Once you have identified these you can start to comment on them to 'get on the radar' of the blog owner. Be a useful member of the community. Check the blogs of the people who comment. Start to network online.

Try to bring your blog to life and involve your followers. Using video in your blog is a brilliant way to create compelling and useful content. Choose whether to use screen capture tools like Owen or hints and tips videos like Richard. Presentations (Owen) and public speaking (Jennifer) also make great content that your followers will enjoy and recommend.

Once you have started to get to know your community better, why not introduce yourself. Remember how Jennifer used LinkedIn to reach out to the business community?

Once you have a relationship established, consider performing video interviews over the internet using Skype and a recording tool. These are extremely cheap and easy to create and they will give you loads of great content (don't forget to transcribe the commentary).

Follow up with people who comment on your blog and always encourage comments and participation. You should aim to bring your blog to life.

There are also lots of other places where you can demonstrate your knowledge. LinkedIn and Facebook have loads of active Groups where you can take part in the conversation as Emma discovered. Look for local groups or ones that are focused on your area of expertise where your experience can be put to use and you can help others as well as learn new ideas yourself.

Don't be frightened to ask questions as well as answer them. It's like socialising in real life - a question is a great way to start a conversation.

When you are ready, why not create your own groups. Being the 'head of the tribe' does have its advantages as Owen, Stephen and Jennifer discovered.

But LinkedIn is not just about potential customers. Remember how Stephen used LinkedIn to find new suppliers and distributors.

Remember also how Stephen used Social Media like Richard and Owen to become an Authority figure? If you have your blog and you are supporting it with video then there is no reason why you can't become an authority figure too.

Your industry doesn't have authority figures? Great! Why not claim it for yourself?

Your industry already has authority figures? Great! There's room for one more then!

Take Jennifer's example. She moved up the ranks from contributor through to trusted source until she has become an industry authority. Now that she has achieved this status she is able to use Social Media to promote herself via Joint Ventures with other Players. She often packages her content into info products as well as gathering hundreds of guests who will pay to hear her speak at live events.

Remember that Social Media is also a double edged sword. If people criticise you then this can be amplified many times over. Always take care to avoid rising to the bait if you are criticised. Just rise above it. Of course, take care to put your side of the story across especially if you feel that the criticism is unjustified, but try to avoid an online punch up or criticising others - it will reflect badly on you.

One final point is about self-promotion. Your knowledge and expertise are your best calling cards. With the exception of paid adverts, Social Media is not about promoting yourself.

Social Media is about people knowing, liking and trusting you.

Keep this in mind and you will be fine.

Before we move on to Dave's view on Social Media, if you would like to stay in touch with us and get access to our latest hints and tips to help you grow your business using the following social media channels, we would love to hear from you and how you're getting on:

Pickaweb Blog: www.pickaweb.co.uk/blog/
Facebook: www.facebook.com/pickaweb.co.uk
Twitter: twitter.com/pickaweb
Pilar on LinkedIn: http://uk.linkedin.com/in/pilartorresw
Tony on LinkedIn: http://uk.linkedin.com/in/tonymesser
Google+: www.pickaweb.co.uk and click on G+ icon
YouTube: www.youtube.com/user/webhostinguk

Dave's View on Social Media

Dave is definitely onto a winner and he knows it! Not only is he a regular blogger now, he has also started to identify some new channel partners to promote his products to their customers. Social media is perfect for this.

Likewise we hope that you too can see the potential and you can see that despite all of the froth and frivolity of social media, there is an amazing opportunity for you to reach out to customers, prospects, suppliers, distributors, partners and a whole range of people or businesses that you could be working with.

More importantly, we are just at the beginning of the whole social media boom and you are in a great position to turn this to your advantage.

Next up, mobile websites.

Action Plan

1. Define your Social Media Profile.
2. Consider your Social Media Role.
3. Create a Social Media Plan for your business based on your Profile and Role.
4. Identify the influential bloggers in your industry, niche or market and subscribe to their blogs.
5. Study their content and make a note of any ideas.
6. Identify non-competing blogs (i.e. not your main competitors but blogs in related areas to your own) and start to comment on their posts. Identify non-competing blogs (i.e. not your main competitors but blogs in related areas to your own) and start to comment on their posts. Feel free to comment on our blog which is a friendly, positive place to get you started. You can find our blog at www.pickaweb.co.uk/blog/
7. Get to know the people that comment on the blogs by visiting their websites and commenting on their blogs where appropriate.
8. Ramp up your own blogging efforts and make your blog a lively place by encouraging audience participation.
9. Sign up for LinkedIn, Facebook, Twitter and YouTube.

10. Create a Facebook Fan Page.
11. Link your blog to your social media accounts.
12. To get an initial following ask existing customers, contacts, suppliers and partners to follow you.
13. Participate in Questions and Answers to demonstrate the depth of your knowledge. Where appropriate use your answers as the basis for blog content.
14. Whenever possible use video as well and embed to your blog posts. Try screen capture, head shots, presentations or any other format you feel comfortable with. Use a Smart Phone too if appropriate.
15. Start to think about how you can pull blog posts together to create longer reports which can be given away for free. We will come back to this shortly.
16. Ask influential bloggers if you can perform a video interview using Skype which you can record and use for content. Transcribe the text for your blog too. It is MUCH easier than it sounds and people are often happy to talk about their expertise.
17. Create a Group in LinkedIn or Facebook. Become the 'Head of the Tribe'.
18. Consider writing a book using your blog posts to establish yourself as an 'Industry Authority' – if you don't maybe your competitors will! You may need a writing coach to help you, but it is worth it.
19. Use Social Media to identify new suppliers, new distributors and joint venture partners.

When Mobiles (Will) Rule The World!

Until recently, the idea of having a mobile version of your website was a bit like having a 'normal' website in the late 1990's. It seemed to be reserved for cutting-edge businesses.

The advent of smart phones, tablet computers, 4G networks and widespread Wi-Fi availability has meant that the biggest growth in terms of Internet access is via mobile devices.

To try to put this all into some perspective let's consider the following figures from Network giant Cisco who estimate that there will be an eighteen-fold growth in global mobile internet traffic between 2011 and 2016. Eighteen-fold! Now that is game changing!

The bottom line is, that mobile is where the action is going to be in the coming years and to put it simply - you need to be there.

As with most of the things discussed in this book, please do not feel that you have missed the boat. We are just at the beginning of the whole Internet revolution, so don't panic.

However, the main reason you need a mobile version of your website is because your website is typically designed to be viewed on a desktop or laptop, with the relevant screen resolutions.

If you try to view most people's websites via a mobile device, you will find that it is not a very satisfying experience. Typically the screen will appear cluttered, text will be hard to read, and the navigation will be virtually impossible.

Mobile Website Builders

Thankfully there are a range of excellent, low cost mobile website building tools available for you. Simply go to http://www.pickaweb.co.uk/lazywebsitesyndrome and click on the Resources link to see one.

Whilst there are restrictions, in terms of size, there are loads of options which make mobile browsing of your website a fulfilling experience for the user. The main point is, that your Mobile Website should act as an entry point for your company. It is not intended to replace your main website, but to complement it.

When people are in the comfort of their own home, or if they are at the office, they are far more likely to find you via their laptop, desktop or tablet device. However, if they are out-and-about and they suddenly need to find you, or they discover you via a search in Google, then your Mobile Website is there for them.

In fact, you can even set up your normal website so that it will automatically detect if the person accessing your site is using a mobile device, and it will present them with the mobile version rather than the full, desktop version.

Here are some of the features of a typical Mobile Website Builder:

- ✓ Find Us - Google map and directions
- ✓ Shopping Cart - Let your customers choose products and buy online
- ✓ About us - One click and customers know about you
- ✓ Opening hours - Tell customers when you are open

for business
- ✓ Reviews - Add reviews from popular review sites
- ✓ Social networking - Let your customers connect with you on Twitter, Facebook, and LinkedIn
- ✓ Call us - One click for your customers to call you
- ✓ Call me back - Call your customers back
- ✓ Reservations - Let your customers request a reservation
- ✓ Coupons - Send customers details of your special offers

Dave's View on Mobile Websites
Using a mobile to access the web is a new one on Dave. He thought they were just for talking. But there are none so holy as the converted and Dave is soon on the case to make sure that he doesn't miss out on that extra mobile traffic.

Action Plan
If you want to stay ahead of your competitors, then have a look at Pickaweb's Mobile Website Builder at our Resources Page link which you can find at www.pickaweb.co.uk/lazywebsitesyndrome - this will allow you to quickly and easily create a mobile website for your business.

Chapter 3: Step 2 - Convert

The Joy of Text

Now that you have optimised your website to attract more traffic, it would be easy to assume that the orders will start to increase.

However, that may not be enough. Having a successful Internet strategy will and this consists of two principal components:

1. Traffic – attracting visitors
2. Conversion – converting visitors into customers

Have you ever wondered how some websites can really capture your attention? They seem to answer all the questions that you have in mind, and you end up either signing up for their free report, or buying something there and then.

A well written website can make the difference between success and failure, and we're going to focus on this crucial issue.

So, we are going to focus on the actual text of your site, or as it is often referred to as, your website's 'copy'. We will look at a simple formula that can quickly and easily improve it, and we will show you what motivates your customers to buy and why you need to ensure that your copy reflects this.

Bounce Rate

Previously, we recommended that you should install Google

Analytics. One of the things that this powerful tool allows you to see is how successful you are at maintaining people's interest. This is known as your website's 'Bounce Rate'. (If you have not installed it yet, we really advise that you do, refer back to that section to find out how.)

JARGON BUSTER: *Bounce Rate is a calculation that represents the percentage of visitors who come to your website and then 'bounce' (i.e. leave the site) without visiting another page. In short, you have just a few precious moments to convince them of the merits of your site.*

The higher the percentage bounce rate, the less interested they are in what you have to offer. We will show you some powerful ways to reduce the bounce rate, but one of the quickest ways to address this, is to spend some time focusing on your copy.

AIDA

How can you achieve this? Well, for more than a century, marketing experts have used the acronym AIDA to express a method of helping customers to make the decision to buy.

This stands for:

- ✓ Attention
- ✓ Interest
- ✓ Desire
- ✓ Action

E. St. Elmo Lewis was the first person to come up with this formula, back in 1898. The amazing thing is that it still works today!

Let's look at each of these in turn:

Attention

If you have something on your website that makes a visitor stay on your page long enough to read something, then you have their attention.

Most visitors have not arrived by accident. Usually, they have found you through a search engine because you have understood how to identify the best Keywords. Maybe a friend or colleague has referred them. The key thing to remember is, that you have what they are searching for, whether it is a physical item, a service or some useful information.

Now, there are lots of theories about website layout and advanced advertising, but one key element is to make sure that you have a clear and concise headline, which grabs your visitors' attention. You have a couple of seconds maximum, to make an impact, so make it easy and quick to understand. This is often referred to as the 'Strapline'.

There are no hard and fast rules about Straplines, but remember that at this stage we want to grab the attention of our audience. We recommend keeping it short - say up to five or six words. Make it positive and upbeat, and ensure that it identifies the advantages or benefits that you offer.

Positioning your Strapline is important too. An expression that is often used is 'Above the fold'. This is an old newspaper expression to make sure that the headlines were shown above the line where the newspaper was folded. This applies to web pages too, and the trick is to make sure that people do not have to scroll down to see your message.

Interest

OK, so hopefully you've written a great Strapline, which will gain your visitor's attention. Now we need to raise their interest even further by putting them in the driving seat. By this, we mean you need to answer that vital question that is in the mind of potential customer: "What's in it for me?"

You need to quickly identify the key selling points of your service to back up your Strapline. This enables the customer to start visualising themselves using what you have on offer. Several concise bullet points should suffice, but they must be credible and to the point - you must engage people, not bore them with details about you!

Desire

Now you need to build on your viewer's interest and create a level of desire. Again, remember that most people have not arrived by accident. They are here for a reason. You have something that they want or need, and you can provide a solution for them. It is at this point that you need to appeal to their emotions and needs.

The most effective way to do this is to identify the benefits of your product, service or organisation. A common mistake at this point is to identify a great, long list of product features. Whilst these are important, they do not appeal emotionally to people in the same way that benefits do.

For example, would you choose the dentist who tells you that he has the sharpest drill or the one who promises you the Hollywood smile? Of course we take it as given that our dentist has a full set of clean, sharp tools, but it is the final result, that Hollywood smile, that we are more interested in.

A really easy way to identify your benefits is to first write down a list of features of your product or service. Then for each one, try to identify what benefit that feature offers your customer. Try to convert cold features into warm benefits. Think ease of use, practicality, beauty, grace, time saving or anything else that you feel, expresses the advantages of the product or service that you provide.

In terms of presentation, some people prefer bullet points and others prefer paragraphs. Again, there are no hard and fast rules, but whatever you choose, keep them concise, engaging and positive.

Useful Tip: One really powerful technique, which works well, is to speak actively to your audience. Tell your potential customers what your product or service will do for them. Use the word 'WILL' to tell them of the effect of using your product or service.

For example:

- ✓ You will look better
- ✓ You will work better or faster
- ✓ You will achieve greater profits
- ✓ Our Service will ensure that...

Once you have the customer imagining the benefits of your product or service, they will want to investigate further, they will want to see the features of your product and it is at *this* point that you can start to explain what those are. Refer to other pages, or to your Blog if necessary to elaborate the product features in greater detail.

Action
Your customers are paying attention, they are interested and they want your product. Now you want them to *take action!*

Here is where your 'Call To Action' comes into play. Your customers should not have to search around the page (or worse yet, the whole website) to find the place where they can order your products.

So include phrase like this:

- ✓ Buy now!
- ✓ Order now!
- ✓ Click here to start your free 30-day trial
- ✓ Access Your Free Copy Here

If your website does not have an online shopping facility, then your 'Call to Action' should describe exactly what is required, such as:

1. Call us toll free now on 0800 123456
2. Click here to request an instant call back
3. If you use a chat facility then say, "Click here to chat to one our customer representatives"

Useful Tip: Make the 'Call To Action' easy to follow, and easy to find. If you can have it on the first page they visit, then that is even better. BUT do not give them too many options either - give people too many choices and they will do nothing! So test which 'Call To Action' works best, and use that - you will be amazed at the results.

Dave's View on Website Copy
Now we are firmly on Dave's territory. He loves a good sales

pitch and he knows that the headline is a vital component to capture people's attention.

He soon has a few variations to try out and he is keen to see which call to action gets him the best results.

Action Plan

1. Check Google Analytics and see what your Bounce Rate is (or install it if you haven't done so already!).
2. Create a positive upbeat headline for your website *(attention)* and keep it 'Above the Fold'.
3. Back up your headline with several bullet points *(interest)*. Tell your visitors 'what's in it for them'.
4. Tell your visitors how you will positively impact their lives or their situation *(desire)*.
5. Include a 'Call to Action' *(action)* that tells them exactly what they need to do to obtain your product or service.
6. Repeat on other relevant pages of your website.
7. Regularly check your bounce rate.

Are You For Real?

OK, you've got a great Strapline, your visitors are warming up to you, and they like the products or services that you offer. They want to find out more about you.

Now their mind switches to another vital component of the sales process - trust.

Shortly, we will show you why educated customers are far more responsive to you, and we will show you how to achieve this, but first they need some proof - they need to know that they can trust you.

There are three really quick ways to develop trust, and that is by displaying the following prominently on all main pages of your website:

1. Customer Testimonials; which show how well you have performed for your previous customers.
2. Professional, Industry or Trade Accreditations; to demonstrate that you have attained the recognised professional level in your field.
3. Key Suppliers Logos; which demonstrate the level of quality of the suppliers that you use.

Let's have a look at them in more detail.

Customer Testimonials

The golden rules of Customer Testimonials are:

- If you don't ask, you won't receive. Do not be shy. You'll be pleasantly surprised at how willing people are to provide feedback, especially long-term clients.

- They MUST be genuine. It is fine to suggest that they include a certain phrase, but NEVER be tempted to make them up.
- They MUST be approved. Just because somebody sent you a thank you email, does not mean that you have their permission to use it. Again, just ask politely.
- Try not to use the same one over and over again. People will spot it. They may think it is the only one you have!
- If you can get them to appear in a video, this will add even more impact. Nothing flash, just a quick thank you on a smartphone or laptop video will be perfect.

Finally, why not contact ALL your suppliers, and ask if you can provide a testimonial for their website with a link back to your website. We will come on to link building shortly, but this is an EASY way to get good, relevant links, and often your suppliers will have a good ranking website!

Professional, Industry or Trade Accreditations

If you are in an industry that requires a level of professional accreditation, then it is vital that you demonstrate this. Whether you are an accountant, a financial adviser, an architect, a builder, a linguist, therapist or any other type of professional, then it is likely that your prospective clients are aware of these qualifications.

Display these prominently, because if not they are unlikely to take you seriously, and consequently 'bounce' off your website.

Key Suppliers Logos

Who are your suppliers? Whose products and services do you

use? Are your customers or prospective customers likely to recognise them? Some suppliers may be household names, whereas others may be recognised leaders to those in your particular market or industry.

Either way, you should clearly list your top suppliers where appropriate, and include their logo clearly on your website. This infers a higher level of quality by association with your brand.

One way to successfully achieve this, is to show your suppliers´ logos slightly faded out rather than in full colour, and listed in a horizontal bar across your website. In terms of positioning, they do not necessarily need to take pride of place at the top of your page but placing them halfway down, just below the 'fold' will be fine.

Dave's View on Testimonials, Accreditations and Supplier Logos

"Testimonials? Why didn't you say so before?" asks Dave. In fact, he keeps getting them in Facebook for a start.

As for suppliers and accreditation, that's easy. Dave is an old hand in the industry and he's always keen to tell everyone about who he works with. He just didn't think it was worth putting on the website.

Action Plan

1. Contact several of your regular customers, and ask for a Testimonial, or check back in your emails to see if you can find one. Remember, that often customers will be happy to offer a testimonial when they have received good service.

2. If your company or any of your staff are accredited, make sure that these are displayed prominently on your website to demonstrate that you are a professional organisation.
3. Do you have suppliers that are household names? If so, use their logos on your website (with their permission if necessary).

It's Good to Chat

If you have a website for your business and you are serious about attracting new visitors, or keeping existing customers happy, then a chat facility is a no-brainer.

In fact, at our UK web hosting business Pickaweb, we have been using an online chat tool since we started and to be honest it is probably the number one conversion tool.

If you do not have a chat tool on your website, then you are at a serious disadvantage to those of your competitors who do.

If your competitors do not use a chat tool, then you could be about to get a massive advantage over them.

The benefits of having Live Chat on your website are:

- ✓ Live Chat says that you are open for business and that you are serious about Customer Service.
- ✓ It gives a sense of security that you are there for your customers.
- ✓ Customers prefer the anonymity of online chat. It is a fantastic way to encourage them to engage with you.
- ✓ People sometimes feel intimidated speaking to someone over the phone and they are more comfortable asking questions over a chat tool, especially if it is regarding a product or service that they do not understand.
- ✓ It is free to the client.
- ✓ Is extremely efficient - your staff can handle several

chats at once, rather than one phone call at a time.
- ✓ It's cheap.
- ✓ With some chat systems customers can chat to you via their Smart Phone.
- ✓ It allows you to capture their email address.
- ✓ It's easy to install.
- ✓ It's a fantastic way to train new staff - some have chat monitoring features for supervisors.
- ✓ It encourages consistent sales messages by the use of canned response.
- ✓ You can create different departments, and route chats through to them, e.g. Sales, Accounts, Tech Support, Customer Service, etc.
- ✓ It can link into certain help desk tools.
- ✓ It allows managers to identify problems by reviewing chat transcripts.
- ✓ It encourages quick follow-up - "Let me quickly email that over to you" or "If you let me have your number I will arrange for someone to call you straight away".
- ✓ Real Time analysis of your visitors - see how they are finding you, which pages they have visited already, etc.

Of course, there are downsides to using Live Chat. If your Live Chat is always offline, then this can send a negative message. Try to ensure that at least one member of staff is available to answer chats during business hours, even if they only take messages and pass them on to other members of staff to attend to later. In some chat tools, you can even set it not to display the chat facility when you are not connected.

Overall though, once you start using a chat tool you will very quickly see the benefits.

There are a wide variety of website chat tools available. We have prepared a list of the options available to you at our Resource Page at www.pickaweb.co.uk/lazywebsitesyndrome

Dave's View on Live Chat
Dave loves that chat tool on the website.

It frees up his time because he can get one of the junior sales team to respond to initial enquiries. He knows that because he has set up some canned responses that these customers will always receive a consistent set of sales messages.

More often than not people are directed to the company blog so that they can learn more about what they have to offer.

Action Plan

1. Consider if a chat feature is right for your business. If you do, assign a member of your team to be responsible for taking chats.
2. If you decide to use chat, prepare a list of frequently asked questions to pre-populate the system, so that you give standardised responses.
3. Remember to log the details of people who contact you via chat, and follow up with them if necessary, by phone, email or direct mail.

24 x 7 is greater than 8 x 5

Having a 24-hour live answering service suddenly puts even the smallest business in a different league from competitors who do not have this feature.

Even better, it is easy to set up and it is a powerful and cost effective conversion tool.

Even the most dedicated business person cannot be in two places at once, and available 24/7, so missing calls is inevitable.

Voicemail helps, but too often makes you look small and unprofessional - just how many people hang up at the first squeak of an answer phone?

When you consider that up to 70% of callers hang up on hearing voicemail, it makes sense to ensure that all callers are given the courtesy of having their calls answered by a real person and in your company name.

When you factor in that most of these callers are potential new customers, (existing customers are more talkative on voicemail, as they already have a relationship with you) and you consider your Lifetime Customer Value, (we'll cover this shortly) then these really are compelling reasons to set this up.

You can see this type of service at www.pickaweb.co.uk/live-answering-service.htm and that the costs are not prohibitive.

How does the service work?

With this type of service you are assigned a unique telephone number, which you control via an online login area.

You login and set your company name and email address, so that messages can be emailed to you (and optionally your mobile number, so that an SMS can be sent to you when a message is received).

You can redirect your company number to the Live Answering service when you are not available (e.g. out of hours) or even set it as the overflow number when your phones are all engaged.

Any calls passed to the Live Answering Service will be answered in your company's name. The receptionist will explain that nobody is available to speak to them at the moment, but if they would like to leave a name, phone number and a short message they will be called back as soon as possible.

The receptionist will then send you an email and SMS message with full details of the caller and their message, which you can call back when available.

Your ability to allow your prospects and customers to speak to a real person 24/7 will create a professional, can-do image of your company, which makes a 24-hour answering service *extremely powerful* in your conversion toolbox.

Dave's View on 24-Hour Phone Lines
What a brilliant, brilliant idea thinks Dave.

He knows that customers do not keep regular hours and he knows the power of 24*7 and he loves the way that he can capture potential sales leads out of hours much more effectively than his competitors. They must think that Dave's team spend a fortune on a 24 hour sales rota. If only they knew!

Action Plan

Check out a 24-hour answering service like the one we've set up in our Resources Page at www.pickaweb.co.uk/lazywebsitesyndrome

Helpdesk = Sales Desk

Just by moving away from PC based emails, where everyone responds to everyone, to a centrally managed email helpdesk tool, you will IMMEDIATELY experience a HUGE improvement in sales and customer satisfaction.

Why? Look at the potential improvements:

- Central visibility of all important emails - no more sales leads getting lost in staff inboxes
- Faster response times
- Less confusion - assign emails to staff members and reduce duplicated/contradictory responses being sent
- Faster, better quality customer service - auto responder confirms receipt to the sender, and can assign unique ticket ID for easier tracking and reference
- Better management information - central reporting improves understanding of volumes of email and their profile
- More consistent responses through the use of templates
- Better prioritisation - give crucial support issues for key clients or hot new leads priority over lower priority responses
- Searchable database of emails, to identify previous issues for a particular client or issue
- Better security - back up one single database rather than dozens of PCs
- Scalable - new employees can be set up quickly and easily

- Browser based - keep in contact with crucial issues from any Internet connected device
- Better Reporting - manage your email workload better and identify trends and opportunities or issues that need addressing

There are a wide variety of helpdesk tools available. We have prepared a list of the options available to you which you can see by clicking on the Resources link at www.pickaweb.co.uk/lazywebsitesyndrome

Some of these tools will even link up with your Twitter and Facebook accounts so that you can keep all of your communications in one convenient place.

Dave's View on a Central Help Desk

Now that things are really starting to pick up Dave is keen to make sure that nothing falls between the cracks. This could be Dave's best year in terms of sales and he knows that every little detail matters. Having a central helpdesk in place offers him so many advantages. He loves the way that he can login to one central place wherever he is and keep on top of all of his enquiries.

He has also started to use the Knowledgebase built into the system to allow his customers to find what they are looking for.

He also uses the canned responses that are built into the helpdesk to ensure that he can respond quickly and consistently to any enquiries he receives.

He just can't imagine how he managed before. Then he

remembers that he wasn't managing before, he was just responding to whoever appeared at the top of his inbox.

Action Plan

1. Review the helpdesk tools to see if there is one that would suit your needs.
2. Identify how many users you would need to add to the system.
3. Implement a central helpdesk and gain control of your emails.

Lights, Camera, Action!

If a picture paints a thousand words, what can Video do?

The increasing popularity of video sharing sites like Youtube, Vimeo and Viddler, alongside the growth of high bandwidth broadband, and the dramatic rise of low cost, high quality digital video cameras and smart phones, has meant that anyone can become an overnight Internet video sensation.

But Video is more than just an amusing distraction. It is an extremely effective method of attracting visitors to your website and it is a very powerful conversion tool.

Another common misconception is that Video must be expensive, and/or it needs to be extremely polished and professional. Sure, there are some instances where companies need slick promotional videos, but these tend to be corporate-type enterprises with a bigger budget. The truth is, anyone with a hand-held digital video recorder, or even a smartphone can create great, quick videos and have them up on Youtube and their Blog, within minutes.

Videos do not need to be scripted or very long. These days, people enjoy the 'home made' look, and they are happy to overlook the lack of a script, as long as they get the information or advice that your video promises them.

Let's look at a couple of examples to help give you some inspiration.

Behind the Curtain - Hints and Tips Videos

The 'Tricks of the Trade' are a great way for you to quickly and easily create a whole range of useful video content. These will act as gentle pointers to your website, as they create a positive impression in the mind of the viewer.

The great thing about this type of video is there are loads of opportunities for most service providers. Think of a plumber, who is showing you how to fix a dripping tap, or a gardener showing you how to fix a lawn mower.

These types of video can be captured quickly and easily on a smartphone, and without the need for expensive lighting or sound equipment.

Useful Tip: One thing to bear in mind is to avoid shooting all of your arrows at once. If you have several points to cover, then break them down into smaller, bite size videos. This way you will have even more content, and have the chance to add more Keywords to your videos when you upload them to YouTube (more on video SEO in a moment).

Screen Capture

If you have a product or service that can be delivered in digital format, then screen capture tools are a fantastic way to showcase them. Cheap and easy to use, they allow you to record your screen, while giving a running commentary so that you can describe the features of your product or service.

Why not take a look at some of these examples by visiting www.pickaweb.co.uk/lazywebsitesyndrome, just click on Resources and go to the Video Section. These tools are also great for creating useful tutorials to help your customers get the best out of your service.

If you are camera-shy, then screen capture tools could prove to be your first step to video heaven! This approach allows you to add your personality to the video, without the need to show your face. Gradually you will discover your true 'voice', and over time appearing on screen will not seem so daunting.

You may initially find that you sound a bit stiff and formal in terms of your delivery. This is natural as there is a tendency in most of us to deliver a 'rehearsed' performance; the trick is to try to be as conversational as possible. Imagine that you are talking to your best friend or a member of your family and they have just asked you to help them understand what it is that you do. This way you will find that you deliver a more relaxed, conversational tone.

Useful Tip: Keep your videos short. Some tools will limit you to five minutes, which is a really useful way of ensuring that you condense everything down to the most important points.

Unfortunately, there is a temptation to ramble on, but remember people's attention spans are pretty short if your video is a monologue. The exception to this rule are for things like video interviews where there is an interesting two way conversation. If you do have a subject that you wish to cover in depth you may want to consider making several videos, rather than one long one.

Whiteboard

Some people will jump at the chance to get their marker pens out and start drawing on the office whiteboard. If that is you, then maybe a whiteboard video approach would be perfect for you.

Choose your subject, write a few main headings in different colours and, hey presto, you even have your headings to remind you what to cover.

This type of approach is perfect if you need to illustrate certain points, with the freedom to create diagrams or flow charts.

Lighting and sound may be a consideration here, but try not to get too hung up about this. A reasonable lapel microphone isn't expensive, but make sure that your camera does have the red microphone jack so that you can record your voice directly into the camera to ensure better quality.

The Headshot

Once you have the confidence to star in your own videos, then 'Headshots' are a great way to do this.

Some people are natural, and they have no problem delivering a 10-minute monologue with no prompting.

However, if you feel that you lack the confidence to deliver off the cuff videos, then you can use a low-cost autocue tool. There are loads of these available and some are free. You simply enter your text and set the speed of the text moving up the screen. Just place your laptop or screen underneath the camera, but try to get it as close as close as possible.

Useful Tip: Remember to look the camera in the eye and talk to your audience in a relaxed manner. It will feel strange at first, but persist with it and imagine that you are explaining something to your best friend or a member of your family. Keep looking the camera in the eye – it really makes a difference.

Video for Traffic

OK, so we have established that Video is a great conversion tool because it gives a face and a voice to your company, and it helps to position you as an expert in your field.

But there are three VERY important reasons why you should use video:

1. Video appears in search engine results
2. Video results are far more likely to be clicked on than pure 'text only' results (estimated to be up to 50 times more likely)
3. The competition for video results is MUCH, MUCH lower (e.g. thousands or millions of text results vs. zero, tens or hundreds of video results)

Let's think about that. If you decide to use Video in your website, and you optimise it correctly for your chosen Keywords, and your competitors do not, then you are giving yourself a significant advantage over less savvy competitors.

Video SEO

Whenever you upload a video to YouTube or any other video sharing site, remember to optimise it for search engines. To do this, make sure that you include your Keywords in the title of your video. These are effectively the Metatags of that page so we want to make sure that your video appears when people search on that Keyword.

Also, include a link back to your website at the very top of the Description area so that people clearly see your website, and if they like your video they may come and visit your site.

You will also notice that there is a section in YouTube where you can add 'Tags'. Use this section to add your keywords to help people to find your videos.

Social Video

It is also overlooked that YouTube is also a social platform. Try to interact with your viewers and ask them to subscribe and comment on your videos. The reason for this is because videos that receive a lot of comments will get a higher position in Google search results.

Dave's View on Video

If Dave is honest he only thought YouTube was for laughs. Never in a million years did Dave think he would appear on video (unless it was his holiday in Tenerife).

Now that he can see the potential he is becoming quite an accomplished performer. He has dusted off a few old sales pitches and brought them to life to demonstrate the benefits of his company and their services. He knows he won't win any Oscars for his performances, but he might win some new business.

Action Plan

1. Consider which video strategy is right for you: hints and tips, screen capture, whiteboard or head shot?
2. Have a bit of fun making a few practice videos and see how you improve.
3. Post your video on YouTube and link back to your website.
4. If you post your video to your website make sure you update your sitemap in Google Webmaster Tools.
5. Check our resources page for more hints and tips on video:www.pickaweb.co.uk/lazywebsitesyndromehints

Talkers are Hawkers and Writers are Experts

Short for electronic books, eBooks are the digital media equivalent of their printed counterparts. A free eBook, which provides comprehensive information about a topic related to your niche, can convince interested visitors to sign up for your marketing messages.

While eBooks demand more time and resources than newsletters, they are a great giveaway for marketers who have specialised industry knowledge, or can provide users with comprehensive information about their subject. Free eBooks are usually 20 to 70 pages in length.

Writing an eBook can seem daunting, but they are a very powerful way of enticing your visitors to give you their contact details. Your eBook should be benefit-oriented, and the title should convey exactly what a reader can expect to gain from it.

The following are some examples of free eBook titles for various industries:

Consultancy:	*13 Killer Guerrilla Marketing Techniques for Your Web Business*
IT:	*59 Tips for Cutting Down IT Costs*
Design:	*How to Design a Web Site That Search Engines Will Love*
Property and Real estate:	*The Art of Home Selling*
Finance:	*10 Proven Strategies for Debt Elimination*
Gardening:	*33 Gardening Secrets from an Award WinningNursery Owner*
Home and garden:	*How to Design Your Own Home Office*

If you do not have the time to write an eBook, why not consider one of the following options instead:

Reports

Reports tend to be shorter and less comprehensive than eBooks. They offer insight into a specific topic in a straightforward and well-organised format and are usually three to 20 pages long.

Free reports should be focused, current and informative. For instance:

Consultancy:	*Brand Management in the Age of Social Media*
IT:	*The Real Costs of Outsourcing*
Design:	*11 Most Common Design Mistakes*
Property and Real estate:	*Success Tactics for Real Estate Investment*
Finance:	*Top 10 Financial Management Tools*
Gardening:	*9 Tips for Container Gardening*
Home and garden:	*Guide to House Cleaning*

White Papers

Another popular format is the White Paper. These are often used in business and politics to educate readers and help them make decisions. White papers are authoritative reports and guides that can be used to provide valuable information to people about your industry, and to establish authority in your market space. White papers are well researched, and logically strong, and are usually created for more targeted niches.

The following are some sample subjects of white papers:

Consultancy:	*Case Study: Internet Marketing for Local Business*
IT:	*IT Investment Guide*
Design:	*Branding Your Website*
Property and Real estate:	*Annual Real Estate Industry Outlook*
Finance:	*Credit Risk Assessment*
Gardening:	*Embracing Innovation in Garden Technology*
Home and garden:	*Environment and Architecture*

Videos

Increasingly, Videos are being used as an important way of engaging with potential customers. They are well suited to the presentation of useful information that would be more difficult in written format, for example technical guides. They also allow a company to have a public face, and can help to reassure potential customers. Recently tools such as Camtasia and Apple's Keynote, mean that anyone can quickly integrate video and presentation tools like PowerPoint, to create engaging video presentations.

The following are some examples of Video use for different sectors:

Consultancy:	*What can Social Media do for Your Business*
IT:	*Comparison of 3 Top CRM tools*
Design:	*The 5 Point Website Makeover Plan*
Property and Real estate:	*The 5 things you Must do to Close a Sale*

Finance:	*The Tax Secrets They do not Want You to Know About*
Gardening:	*How to Prepare a Vegetable Plot*
Home and garden:	*Creating Value in Your Home*

Newsletters

A regularly distributed publication, centred around a specific theme, product or industry. Note that as a giveaway, your newsletter must have more than news about your company, it must also offer valuable insights, tips or information for your readers.

Newsletters are popular because they enable marketers to integrate their messages within the periodic email itself. By creating an effective newsletter, you can greatly improve your open rates and click-throughs, since each newsletter offers your users something of value. Newsletters are also effective for cross marketing.

Newsletter articles should be benefit-oriented and optimised for quick reading. Through your newsletter articles, offer your users insights and advice or solve a common problem.

The following are some sample titles of newsletter articles for various industries:

Consultancy:	*Starting a Company Blog: Is It Worth the Trouble?*
IT:	*Changes in Microsoft's Software Licensing and What it Means for Hosts*
Design:	*What Does Your Logo Say About Your Company?*

Property and Real estate:	*Finding High Potential Investment Opportunities in a Recession*
Finance:	*Setting Your Personal Financing Goals For the Coming Year*
Gardening:	*Prepping Your Garden For Cold Weather*
Home and garden:	*How to Choose A Hardwood Floor*

CD-ROMs, DVDs or Other Physical Gifts

While such gifts have an added cost of developing and shipping, they can be some of the most effective ways to build a subscription. CD-ROMs and DVDs of training videos, and other learning material, can help your business establish credibility and loyalty, and give your email marketing an immediate edge.

Consultancy:	*Training Video for Building Customer Relations*
IT:	*Free Trial Software*
Design:	*CD/Download Pack: 7 Free Customisable Templates*
Real estate:	*DVD: Social Marketing Secrets for Real Estate Investors*
Finance:	*Training Course On Forex Trading*
Gardening:	*Gardening Calendar*
Home and garden:	*Free Custom Stencils for House Painting*

Useful Tip: If you really like the idea of an eBook, but not sure where to start, then try a report first, then expand on that to make an eBook. Also you can harvest information from your Blog, and re-word it into a fantastic eBook, simply create a plan, map out your sections and get writing!

OK, so we hope you can see that as an expert in your field, you have something extremely valuable to offer prospective customers for free - put it in writing and offer it to your customers, do not be afraid to show your knowledge and expertise.

But that is just the start, next we will show you how you can give your Free Gift (eBook, report, whitepaper etc.) away *in return for someone's email address.* As you will see, it is an inexpensive and extremely easy way to get this valuable information, and we will show you how to set it up and put onto autopilot so you can focus on other areas of your business.

Dave's View on Free Giveaways
Dave has always been happy to leave some promotional material with his customers, but this is something different altogether.

Now his approach is to identify a need that his potential customers have and to write a report that addresses this head on. He knows the market inside out so he knows which questions his prospective clients have. He finds that an educated prospect is much more likely to choose him than a competitor who is probably just trying to sell on price alone.

In the next section we show you how to harvest sales on autopilot using your Free Gift.

Action Plan

1. Consider what you can offer your customers for free. Focus on their needs and concerns rather than trying to sell yourself.
2. Think about the best way to deliver your Free Gift. Can it be delivered digitally for instant gratification or do you need to mail it?

Chapter 4: Step 3 - Grow

Harvesting vs. Hunting

In this section, we will introduce a very powerful technique called 'Follow-Up Marketing'. We strongly recommend that you introduce this technique as a key element of your marketing strategy, because it will have a dramatic effect on your level of sales.

We will show you why the old business model just doesn't cut it today. We will show you how you can stay in your customers mind so that they think of you when they are ready to buy. We will also show you which pitfalls to avoid and examples to use.

Online Business – The Old Way

OK let's cast our mind back a few years. Traditionally, when someone approached your business, they might have made a few enquiries, you would have provided them with some sales literature, or maybe a sales brochure, and they may or may not have purchased from you. Those days are long gone.

Then along came the Internet, which offered a new way for businesses to sell their goods or services. However, the sales model we just looked at has stayed the same, even if a website was used in place of the sales brochure. Potential customers approach a website, they look around and they may or may not purchase. They have endless possibilities to search through, and it is easy for your voice to be drowned out by those of your competitors.

The key questions that you should be asking yourself are, "How do I stand out from the crowd?" and "How do I manage to get a prospect's attention and retain it long enough to convert them to a full paying customer?"

Follow-Up Marketing – Online Business version 2.0

Well recently, there has been a revolution in the way that companies market their products or services and this is called 'Follow-Up Marketing'.

Basically, it is a technique for ensuring that you maintain a consistent, and repetitive sales message, to both prospects and existing customers, which quickly results in a dramatic increase in conversions, from prospects to customers and it is neither expensive, nor complicated to implement.

In fact, as well as allowing you to sell more, it will also free up your time, which will allow you to concentrate on working on the business, rather than in it, and it will have a massive effect on your profitability.

When do Customers Buy?

The real power of 'Follow-Up Marketing' is that is allows you to stay in the forefront of the mind of potential and existing customers. The reason that this is absolutely fundamental to your success is that 'customers will buy when they are *ready to buy*'. They do not buy when you are ready to make a sale. By implementing 'Follow-Up Marketing' you have the opportunity to deliver a consistent message to your customers.

You are able to convey many positive messages about

yourself, your business, your products and services. You give your prospects the opportunity to remember you, to learn about your offering and your business, to know that you are there for them when they need you, and above all you give them a reason to trust you.

Useful Tip: But remember, do not make your 'Follow-Up Marketing' all about you. Keep in mind WIIFM (What's In It For Me) and make your follow-up messages interesting and informative.

Your Most Important Asset?

Now, you can use this approach for any number of sales angles, and it is especially powerful once you have converted prospects into customers. In fact, *up-selling* to your existing customers must become a central theme of your on-going success, and this approach almost guarantees it. The most valued asset to your company is your database - nurture this and your lifetime value will increase -, which, in turn, increases your yearly profits (we explain how to calculate lifetime value later on).

Why Harvesting Business is much more effective

Harvesting Business is so much easier than hunting for customers. When you understand this principle, you will see that instead of going out 'looking' for new business, customers will be coming to you, OR you have more opportunities to up-sell.

When you adopt the mind-set that it is your mission to capture the contact details of anyone who makes an enquiry, you are then in control and can keep them updated and informed of all your services.

Of course, a great way of doing this is to offer a 'Free Gift' (explained in the previous section) - you simply ask for the visitor's name and email address in exchange for this information.

Do not be tempted to buy email lists. You have no idea where this information has come from, you do not have these people's permission to email them, and it can get you blacklisted for spamming.

Once you have managed to get a few email addresses from genuine sales enquiries (or in exchange for your free gift) the first thing you need to do is to create a Follow-Up Sequence of pre-written emails related to your products or services.

There are no hard and fast rules about the number of follow-ups and their format is not set in stone, so feel free to experiment and use the approach that you feel most comfortable with.

The 'F' Word!!

Before you get started, we have some great ideas that will help you to put the finishing touches to your first 'Follow-Up Marketing Campaign'.

But what happens if you have a business where you cannot sell across the Internet - such as a hotel or restaurant - how can this approach help you? Well recently, many savvy businesses have realised that the Internet offers them a low-cost way to reach out to potential customers, and to maintain them, and that is by the use of the 'F' word. Yes, we are talking about offering something for 'Free'.

Now that you have your eBook or at least have given some thought to your 'Free Gift' you can offer *this* to your clients.

Paco's Tapas Bar

To put this into perspective, let's take an example of a business that might not strike you as being one that can harness the potential of the Internet.

Imagine a local family owned restaurant: 'Paco's Tapas Bar'. It is not part of a large chain, but a small family run restaurant serving traditional Spanish cooking.

They have a small website showing their menus, some photos of Paco and the guys, their contact details, opening times etc. They do not offer home delivery services, and until recently, Paco did not really feel that the Internet offered them too many opportunities, except as a way to advertise their business online.

But it is a great restaurant, and Paco was getting so many requests from his customers for this or that recipe, that he decided to share some of them on his website.

They were totally free, and Paco was soon getting some great compliments from his existing customers, as well as noticing new faces in the restaurant.

Some of these new customers mentioned that their friend had emailed them a link to the recipe, so they thought they would come in and try the real thing.

Light Bulb Moment #1 - Email the Recipes

Then one day, while he was chatting to one of his customers about his favourite dishes, he offered to go and fetch a couple of recipes that he had out back in his office. "Hey, do not worry", said the customer, "I can see you're busy. Why not just email them over," and handed Paco his email address.

Paco had a light bulb moment! "Why don't I ask these people for their email addresses and I can send them all the details of my dishes by email". A great idea, but soon he found that this was just taking up too much of his time, even though he knew that it was great for business.

Light Bulb Moment #2 - Automate the Sequence

Fortunately, one of his regular customers (who understood email marketing) suggested that Paco automate the process. He suggested that Paco put his recipes together in order, and build a sequence of emails, which could be automatically sent when someone entered in their email address. In return, the visitor would receive a new recipe sent over to their inbox at regular intervals.

Light Bulb Moment #3 - Email Special Offers

But that was just the start. Next Paco noticed that Wednesday was his least busy night so, he introduced a 'Wednesday night special!' He sent a quick email invitation to his list of customers, and suddenly Wednesday evenings were almost as busy as Friday.

From this point on, he had a growing list of eager customers who he emailed in advance of special events and dates, offering promotions, wine tastings, cooking demonstrations, discounts and a whole range of new and exciting services.

A Gift that Never Stops Giving

This is all within the reach of any business. None of this is difficult, complex or expensive. It just takes some imagination and the right tools. The key throughout though, is to build confidence and trust in the eyes of your potential customers, and a really powerful way to achieve this is to give something away for Free.

It might sound a bit strange at first, and of course you need to consider carefully what you are going to give away. In Paco's case, he might not want to give away his most closely guarded culinary secrets, but he is happy to give away details of some of his favourite classic Spanish dishes.

Automating Your Follow-Up

Previously, we looked at your 'Free Gift' as a Conversion Tool. It allows you to demonstrate your expertise, and it helps to position you as the expert in the eyes of your prospects.

In itself, this is a great start, but you've now opened a dialogue with your prospects, and they will be much more receptive to your ideas.

It usually takes several visits to your website before people are ready to buy. (It has been estimated that the actual number of visits is between six to eight!). By automating a sequence of follow-up emails, you become welcome in your prospects' email inbox, and therefore put yourself in pole position when your prospects are ready to buy.

Useful Tip: When you first get your customers email address (in response to a enquiry, or in exchange for your free gift) it is usually wise to state that they are signing up for follow-up emails. This way you cannot be accused of spam - if you are worried about people not wanting to receive any of this information, you should always include a 'un-subscribe' option at the bottom of each message. This is actually a built in feature of most auto-responder tools, as we will shortly see.

If all of this sounds a bit complicated then do not panic! There are specialised tools, which make the creation of automatic sign-up forms, linked to an auto-responder email tool, within the grasp of even the least technically minded person.

Tools like Aweber, Constant Contact, MailChimp, GetResponse and iContact are all good examples of low-cost, but feature rich auto-responder tools. However this subject is a book of its own, so why not check out our Resources Page, which has more information, simply go to; www.pickaweb.co.uk/lazywebsitesyndrome

Another point to consider is that you can also create sequences for prospects (e.g. people who are not yet customers) and existing customers. The advantage is that you can speak to them from a different perspective.

Let's have a look at a couple of examples:

Convert – Example Pre-Sales Sequence

In this example, we will consider a home gardening service. A potential customer has contacted you because they need some help to keep on top of their garden work.

At this stage, you should aim to provide a wealth of free information over a period of time to create trust.

An example pre-sales follow-up sequence may look something like this:

1. Initial follow-up to your enquiry – introduce yourself and ask if they have any questions (Day 1)
2. Send Free E-Report – Gardening Secrets From an Award-winning Nursery Owner (Day 3)
3. Follow-up email – Just checking that you got the report? (Day 7)
4. A quick email with some feedback / testimonials from your existing customers (Day 14)
5. Can I schedule a phone call to discuss your requirement? (Day 21)
6. Free report – improving the soil quality of your garden (Day 28)
7. Free Gardening Calendar (Day 35)
8. Follow-up email – Just checking that you got the Calendar? (Day 42)
9. Monthly follow-ups, e.g. tip of the month

Create Trust and Create Sales

You can see from this example that we are providing useful and interesting information. The emphasis is not on pricing, but on creating trust. We are trying to convey a sense that we have a great deal of knowledge in our chosen field.

In this case we are providing useful information (Gardening Secrets), some customer feedback, our expertise (soil quality), some branded material (Gardening Calendar) and some useful monthly tips.

By providing potential customers with knowledge, you are offering them something really useful, and you are sowing the seeds for a long and fruitful relationship with them.

Useful Tip: Do not overdo it! The aim is not to bombard them into submission, this will only irritate them, and they will end up unsubscribing from your list.

Whilst it is estimated that it can take up to seven or eight visits to a website before a customer will commit themselves, the key to your communication is to create trust in yourself and your business. That is why educating your customers with useful information is so important.

Grow – Example Post-Sales Sequence
Once you have converted a prospect into a customer, you can consider sending a different type of message.

More advanced Customer Relationship Management tools allow you to set the prospect to not receive more 'pre-sales' emails.

The reason for this is that you can now engage in a different conversation with them. They now trust you, as they are now a client, you can focus on developing your relationship with them, as well as up-selling them to other products and services.

An example post-sales follow-up sequence may look something like this:

1. Initial check that everything is OK with the service (Day 5)
2. Customer Satisfaction Survey (Day 10)*
3. Some Great offers from our local Partners (Day 20)
4. Could we use you as a Customer Reference? (Day 30)
5. Could you 'Like' us on Facebook? (Day 40)
6. Some additional services that may be of interest to you (Day 50)
7. Claim Your Free Gift – range of free sign-up options (Day 60)
8. We have not spoken for some time – let me know a convenient time to call (Day 70)
9. This report may be of interest to you (Day 80)

* You could use an online Survey Tool like http://surveymonkey.com

In this case we are using our sequence to cover a range of factors such as:

- Customer satisfaction (1, 2, and 8)
- Referrals to Partners (3) – in this case we need to be sure that we are on the partners email lists too
- Testimonial Request (4)
- Social Proof (5)
- Identifying needs (6, 7)
- Affiliate Marketing (9)

The theme is completely different from the pre-sales

sequence, and it is aimed at ensuring that you are getting feedback from the client, as well as trying to identify other services that the customer may be interested in.

Useful Tip: Use different sequences for different sectors of your database. Pre-sales emails for potential clients, and up-selling emails for customers (you can usually spot if you are sending the right message to the right sector by looking at the subject lines of your follow-up emails).

Keep it Personal

In terms of etiquette, it is important when you are putting your emails together, to try to and make them as personalised as possible, as well as being from a named person in your company. This is so that the approach is less formal. Remember, you want to encourage this person to use your services, and to give them every reason to contact you. They are far more likely to respond to a named person, rather than just an email from a company or a department.

Make sure you include all your contact details to make it clear who they should contact, and how they can contact you. You should also include your social media links such as Facebook Fan Page, Twitter, YouTube Channel, LinkedIn and Google+ profiles.

The other key factor is to make sure that it is sent from your main sales email address. It must come from an email address that is accessed frequently, so replies are responded to as soon as possible (this is where a central helpdesk really comes into its own). The last thing you want is to miss a potential sale because you just do not check that mailbox.

You must also include the facility to allow people to unsubscribe (mentioned above). If you use an automatic email management tool like Aweber or Constant Contact this is built in to the software.

If it all sounds a bit too much then be assured that we have lots of useful videos - just head over to www.pickaweb.co.uk/lazywebsitesyndrome and click on the Resources link.

Dave's View on Follow-Up

Follow up is one of those areas that Dave was previously very weak on. He knew that persistence paid dividends but it was difficult keeping track of it. This way he knows that he has a completely automatic and customised system that follows up on his behalf.

He loves it when someone responds to him weeks after the initial contact and says that they would like to talk further with him.

So simple, yet so effective.

In the next section, we look at why it is important to know your customer's lifetime value. We have mentioned this a few times already, but we are going to explain exactly why it is so important.

However, before we do, let's take a look at your Action Plan...

Action Plan

1. Create a pre-sales follow-up sequence of 10 to 15 email subject lines, so that you can easily see the order.
2. Once you have the order, write the emails. Focus on education in the early stages. You are in giving mode initially.
3. Remember to ask if you can contact them and invite them to respond to you.
4. Check our resources page, www.pickaweb.co.uk/lazywebsitesyndrome for more information on the auto-responder tools we recommend, and for videos, which explain how to set them up.

What is it all Worth?

In order to really grow your business it is crucial to understand the Lifetime Value of your Customer.

Lifetime Value is the average spend of your customer, over the time they remain your customer. More crucially, what proportion of this spend is profit.

Some businesses will have only one contact with a client, never to see them again (remember that umbrella that you bought when it started raining?) whereas other businesses will see customers return over and over again, over a course of many years (how often do you change your dentist, hairdresser, accountant, legal representative, etc.).

Calculating Your Lifetime Value

This is really important to know, for one simple reason - once you know this figure, then you can calculate what you are prepared to pay to capture a new client.

It is really a bit of a guesstimate to calculate, but here goes: Average profit per transaction x no. of transactions per year x no. years.

Let's use a hairdresser as an example. Imagine that a lady visits the salon once a month, and the average profit is £50 (OK, we understand, but it is a posh salon). She also gets a manicure, buys a bottle of shampoo and conditioner etc. and she has been a faithful client for five years.

Let's find the Lifetime Value of this client to date:

£50 x 12 visits a year x 5 years = £3,000

But that is only part of the story. This lady has her network of friends, and she has referred at least four of them in that time.

Let's factor that in at the same rate for each friend (assuming that they have been coming each month, for two years on average):

£50 x 12 visits x 2 years x 4 friends = £4,800

So, this client is suddenly worth nearly £8,000 to your business(i.e. £3,000 for the lady plus £4,800 for her friends), in terms of profit.

Once you know your Lifetime Value, you are in a much more informed position, when it comes to deciding your marketing budget.

Suddenly offering something for free looks much more appealing. Why not have a look at the product or service that you offer. Is there a way that you can offer a free trial? Maybe a taster, or a time-limited offer. Calculate the cost of offering this versus the Lifetime Value of a Client. Be sure to take into account the number of people who will try but not buy. This will give you a powerful insight into how much business can be generated by offering a free trial or taster.

Maybe you can offer a free report or eBook as we demonstrated earlier. Aside from the time and materials taken to create your 'Free Offer', the on-going costs are fairly insignificant. If this can help you to attract new customers, then this is a powerful and profitable way to grow your business in the long-term.

Dave's View on Life Time Value

Until now Dave was only focused on the next deal. What Dave has realised is that existing customers are far more willing to offer you more custom if you take care of them. You really are pushing at an open door.

Action Plan

1. Try to calculate the Life Time Value of a client. Do not get too hung up getting it to the nearest penny or cent because it is not an exact science.
2. Take a sample of existing customers who have been with you for several years, and see how much return business they have given you.
3. If your business does not have a recurring revenue stream from your customers (i.e. they make one purchase and then do not purchase again) try to think of ways that you can sell additional services to them, or at least try to get a referral from them.

Your Marketing Calendar

A Marketing Calendar is simply a way for you to record your plans for communicating your offers to your clients in advance. By writing them down, it helps you to focus on what you will be offering throughout the year. A Marketing Calendar does not need to be complex or costly, but will really help you keep on track.

The key point is to have one, and that you aim to follow it as much as possible. Do not make it too complicated, but simply starting one will apply a level of discipline to your marketing efforts, and could make a really big difference to your focus and accountability.

Keep it simple, but do take action.

The Benefits of a Marketing Calendar

Discipline

The main benefit is, that it will help you to be consistent and disciplined in your approach to marketing. Just by creating a plan, you will immediately have an advantage over many of your competitors.

Low Cost

Preparing a Marketing Calendar doesn't need to be expensive, and neither does your form of communication. If you have never really communicated with your prospects or clients before, then maybe a schedule of emails will be sufficient to get you started. The only cost will be your time to sit down and prepare the emails. As your confidence grows you can branch out and try other methods.

Identify What Works

Your Marketing Calendar allows you to develop a clear set of Marketing Communications throughout the year, and it encourages you to test and measure to identify which ones offer the best return on investment.

Consistency

It will also allow all of your employees to play a role in delivering that message. If all of your team understand that this month is going to be 'promotion x' and next month will be 'promotion y' then they will all be able to clearly communicate this to anybody that they come into contact with.

Useful Tip: You can encourage and incentivise everyone in your team to reference your offer wherever appropriate, whether with prospects, or existing customers.

Try Something New

A Marketing Plan is also a great way to gently ease you outside of your comfort zone. If you have never tried sending direct mail to your clients, or used Pay per Click advertising, then maybe this is the time to commit.

Who knows, maybe you discover that just standing up in front of a local Chamber of Commerce meeting to present the ideas from your new eBook generates more new leads than any other form of advertising you currently use.

Can be Seasonal

If you operate in a seasonal business, then maybe you can identify the quiet periods and try to figure out a way of increasing sales in that month or quarter. There is no hard and fast rule here, but maybe you can encourage your customers to purchase a service now (i.e. a check-up) before they actually need it. An example would be a central heating check before winter sets in.

Can Focus on Holidays and Festivities

By planning ahead you can be prepared for all of the seasonal holidays and festivities in your local calendar. Whether it is Valentines, Halloween, Christmas or the local Carnival, there will always be an angle that you can use to generate a theme for your marketing.

Can Work With Joint Venture Partners

Do you have a good relationship with other businesses that you could partner with? Again, this is something that many small businesses overlook. Could you introduce them to your customers and vice versa? Now that you have your eBook and sign-up page, maybe you can get some of their customers to subscribe to your services.

Useful Tip: If you have some trusted partners why not scratch each other's backs?

What does a Marketing Calendar Consist of?

Whether you want a paper-based version, an Excel/Word document or an online tool, your Marketing Calendar can be as simple or as complex as you like.

Try not to get too hung up about how it looks. The important point is that you have an overall plan for the month, quarter or year ahead.

We have provided an example for you to download at www.pickaweb.co.uk/lazywebsitesyndrome - just click on the Resources link. Feel free to use this to get started.

Initially you just need to fill in the gaps. You should try to have an activity scheduled all the time, simply sketch out the detail in a Marketing Activity Worksheet.

An activity can be something that occurs once on a given date (e.g. a workshop, networking event, presentation, etc.) or something, which is on-going throughout a certain period (e.g. Promotional offer, Coupon, Seasonal Special).

Marketing Activity Worksheet

The purpose of this document is to force you to consider the following points and commit them to paper. At the end of the activity you can use this to review your achievement to your initial goals.

Your Marketing Activity Worksheet contains the following detail:

- Timeline (start date and end date)
- Name of campaign
- Sales goal for the activity (e.g. £/$/€x,000 in sales of product y in February)

- Name and value of coupon if required
- Name of partner (if applicable)
- Resources required (people, meeting rooms, equipment, printed material, etc. To be expressed in financial terms)
- Measurability (e.g. We will send two versions of the email/postcard and see which one gets the most conversions at two different landing pages)
- Target population (e.g. existing clients, prospects, direct mail list, Chamber of Commerce List)
- Format (e.g. email, group presentation, postcard, DVD, brochure)
- Date for review of baseline to actual results.
- Lessons learned
- Improvements for next time

The reason that we recommend using a tool such as this, is that too often marketing activities are too 'Scattergun' in their approach. The act of committing your ideas and setting a baseline vs. actual results will help you to create the discipline necessary to constantly improve your marketing activities over time.

Useful Tip: Keep track of what marketing activities work, and what didn't. This way you can repeat the activities that were popular over and over again, and re-think the ones that didn't.

Dave's View on Marketing Calendars

Dave's calendar used to be in his head. That explains why his work was so haphazard. Now that he has a sales funnel that is working on auto pilot through his website, he has the chance to plan things into the future.

And it is the future that Dave is very much focused on rather than making things up as he goes along.

Action Plan

1. Create an initial list of marketing activities that you have planned for the next quarter. Include networking groups and any one-off or on-going activity that you have planned.
2. Identify the gaps and start to fill them in with some initial ideas.
3. Prepare a Marketing Activity Worksheet for the next month. Try to focus on what your goals are, and how you intend to measure this. Go for the quick wins, rather than spending a lot on producing printed materials, etc. Maybe an 'Offer of the Month', sent by email with a coupon so that you can measure the success.

Conclusion

Wow, we have covered a lot of ground haven't we?

The reason that we wrote this book was to help you to develop a dynamic website that will help you to drive your business forward. The moment you understand that your website is far more than just a glorified online business card, and is in fact, a tool to generate leads and to allow you to start educating and communicating with your customers, is the moment that you can really start to take your business forward.

Your website can be the centrepiece of your marketing efforts, and it is vital that you focus your initial effort here. This book clearly shows you how to do this in a step-by-step manner.

We have prepared a handy checklist which can be accessed by clicking on the Resources link at www.pickaweb.co.uk/lazywebsitesyndrome and going to the checklist area.

The Missing Ingredient

The reason that we have called this book the 'Lazy Website Syndrome' is that it is almost like having an illness or an ailment.

We all know the Dave's of this world and the real problem they pose is that they seem to infect everyone around them with their laziness and negative attitude.

We know from personal experience that most people are self-critical enough to look at their website in the context of their business and realise that they need to 'do something' about it.

If that is you then this book provides a clear path for you and your business.

However, there is one missing ingredient that we come across over and over again that holds people back.

There is one thing that no book, set of tutorials, networking events or DVDs can address.

That one single ingredient is called Action.

Unless you make a commitment to take the Action required, then it is likely that one week, one month, one year from now, your website and your business will continue to be lazy and will underperform.

They will fail to deliver the results that you deserve. Simply reading this book is not enough, you need to Action the points we have covered, and DO the things we suggest.

However, time is always an issue. Perhaps you know you need to do all of these things, but you just do not have the time or the energy!

Well, there is an alternative...

Need Some Help to Transform Your Business?

We have covered a lot of ground and now you have a

powerful blueprint which you can use to boost the potential of your business.

We understand that you have a lot on your plate and whilst you understand what it takes to transform your business, it is taking action that really counts.

If you feel that you do not have the time to implement what we have shown you then why not let's do it all for you?

We offer a range of competitively priced services which will enable you to achieve what we have laid out in this book - Prospect, Convert & Grow.

To find out how we can help you just click on the Services link at http://www.pickaweb.co.uk/lazywebsitesyndrome for more details.

Our services are competitively priced and are within the reach of any small business owner.

Our aim is to ensure that you get a quick return on your investment.

If this is something that is of interest, then visit our website at www.pickaweb.co.uk/lazywebsitesyndrome. We would love to hear from you. Give it a try and let's help you take your business to the next level!

All the best,

Tony + Pilar

Pilar and Tony

Why not stay in touch with us and get access to our latest hints and tips to help you grow your business using the following social media channels, we would love to hear from you and how you're getting on:

Pickaweb Blog: www.pickaweb.co.uk/blog/
Facebook: www.facebook.com/pickaweb.co.uk
Twitter: www.twitter.com/pickaweb
Pilar on LinkedIn: http://uk.linkedin.com/in/pilartorresw
Tony on LinkedIn: http://uk.linkedin.com/in/tonymesser
Google+: www.pickaweb.co.uk and click on G+ icon
YouTube: www.youtube.com/user/webhostinguk